End Days

by

Deborah Zoe Laufer

FOUNDED 1830

NEW YORK HOLLYWOOD LONDON TORONTO

SAMUELFRENCH.COM

IMPORTANT BILLING AND CREDIT REQUIREMENTS

Development of END DAYS was supported by the Eugene O'Neill Theater Center, Artistic Director; Wendy C. Goldberg, during a residency at the National Playwrights Conference of 2007. Originally presented by Florida Stage, Louis Tyrrell, Producing Director, Nancy Barnett, Managing Director. The rolling world premiere of END DAYS was partially funded by the National New Play Network's Continued Life of New Plays Fund and was produced by Florida Stage, Phoenix Theatre (Indianapolis) and Curious Theatre (Denver)

In addition, LORT licensees shall be required to include the biography of the Florida Stage (a copy of which is attached hereto as Exhibit C) in all programs.

Wendy C. Goldberg, Artistic Director

presents

End Days

★

DEBORAH ZOE LAUFER

Directed by REBECCA BAYLA TAICHMAN

There will be one 10 minute intermission.

CAST

Nelson	David Ross
Arthur	Peter Friedman*
Sylvia	Caitlin O'Connell*
Jesus/Hawking	Ryan King*
Rachel	Zoe Lister-Jones*
Stage Directions	Lily Feinn

ARTISTIC & PRODUCTION STAFF

Scenic Designer	Rachel Hauck
Lighting Designer	Brian J. Lilienthal
Sound Designer	Matt Callahan
Props Designer	Faye Armon
Dramaturg	Martin Kettling
Assistant Stage Manager	Danielle Monica Long
Assistant Scenic Designer	Alex Calle
Assistant Director	Alexandra Bassett
Assistant Lighting Designer	Susannah Scott
Assistant Sound Designer	Ben Inniger
Light Board Operator	Sophia Giordano
Stage Management Interns	Lauren Hirsh
	Danielle Palliser
Literary Representatives	Juliana Avery
	Allison Kellar Lenhardt

FLORIDA STAGE

Louis Tyrrell
Producing Director

Nancy Barnett
Managing Director

and

Kay and Jim Morrissey
Co-Producer

End Days

By Deborah Zoe Laufer

A NATIONAL NEW PLAY NETWORK WORLD PREMIERE

Scenic & Lighting Design by Richard Crowell
Costume Design by Erin Amico◆
Sound by Matt Kelly

Production Stage Manager: James Danford*

Directed by Louis Tyrrell†

Development of *End Days* was supported by the Eugene O'Neill Theater Center
during a residency at the National Playwrights Conference of 2007.

CAST
(in alphabetical order)

Nelson Steinberg . . . . Scott Borish
Rachel Stein. . . . . Michaela Cronan
Sylvia Stein . . . . Elizabeth Dimon
Jesus / Stephen Hawking . . . . Terrry Hardcastle
Arthur Stein . . . . Jim Shankman

PRODUCTION STAFF

Production Manager	**Richard Crowell**	Musical Consultant	**Tom Kenaston**
Technical Director	**Phillip Schroeder**	Wigs Provided by	**Wigboys**
Assistant Technical Director	**Josh Aune**	Assistant to the Master Electrician	**George Sciarrino**
Prop Master	**Michael Blair**	Assistant to the Stage Manager	**Ashley Simon**
Costume Coordinator	**Erin Amico**	Assistant to the Costume Coordinator	**Leslye Menshouse**
Sound Engineer	**Matt Kelly**	Assistant to the Sound Engineer	**Chris Shafer**
Master Electrician	**Michael Jon Burris**	Scene Shop Assistants	**Aaron Burton**
Crew Chief	**Stephanie Kelly**	Stage Crew	**Aaron Burton, George Sciarrino and Chris Shafer**
Carpenters	**Jim Gibbons, Michael O'Rourke**		
Scenic Artist	**Cindi Blank Taylor**		

◆Member, United Scenic Artists
*Member, Actors Equity Association
†Member, Society of Stage Directors and Choreographers

*The Actors and Stage Manager employed in this stage production are members of Actors Equity Association,
the union of professional actors and stage managers in the United States.*

PHOENIX 🔥 THEATRE

END DAYS

by
Deborah Zoe Laufer

January 3 - February 3, 2008

CAST

Nelson Steinberg	MATTHEW VAN OSS
Sylvia Stein	MARTHA JACOBS*
Arthur Stein	BILL SIMMONS*
Jesus/Stephen Hawking	MATTHEW ROLAND
Rachel	PHEBE TAYLOR*
Stephen Hawking	MATTHEW ROLAND

There will be one 12-minute intermission.

CREW

Director/Set & Light Design	BRYAN FONSECA*
Set Design	JAMES GROSS
Costume Design	KAREN A. WITTING
Sound Design/Original Music	TIM BRICKLEY
Technical Director/Properties	JUSTIN KIDWELL
Stage Manager/Sound/Light Operator	MICHAEL MARSHALL
Set Construction	JAMES GROSS, JUSTIN KIDWELL
	& MICHAEL MARSHALL

*Indicates member of Actors Equity Association
The videotaping or other audio recording of this production is strictly prohibited.

The Phoenix Theatre's Mission

The Indianapolis-based Phoenix Theatre entertains by presenting the best of professional, contemporary theatre in an intimate setting. Engaging our community, patrons, and staff with issue-oriented plays, the Phoenix enlightens audiences about social concerns while challenging them to re-examine their roles in society.

Special thanks to: Gale Nichols, Ted Widlanski, Bill Taylor, Adrienne Reiswerg, Matthew Chaifetz & Lara Schmutte, Rabbi Aaron Spiegel, Tom Swiezy, Larry Williams, Florida Stage

Very special thanks to: J. Scott Keller

The building housing The Phoenix Theatre, built as a First United Brethern Church in 1907, was donated by **J. Scott Keller** in memory of his cousin, **Miss Janet (Genet) Flanner**, member of the American Academy and Institute of Arts and Letters, and Paris correspondent for *The New Yorker* for 30 years.

FLORIDA STAGE BIOGRAPHY

Florida Stage is a not-for-profit professional theatre company that produces exclusively new and developing works in its intimate, 250 seat home in Manalapan, Florida, just south of Palm Beach. The theatre was founded as the Learning Stage in 1985 by award-winning actor/director Louis Tyrell. Over the past two decades, the company has produced more than 125 plays, more than 25 of which have been world premieres.

In addition to its innovative main stage program, the theatre maintains a vibrant education department, offering a full roster of creative, artist-driven programs for students. The theatre also holds an annual new play festival called 1st Stage. Florida Stage has been honored in many ways for its artistic and education efforts, including the Theatre League of South Florida's inaugural Bill Von Maurer Award for Theatrical Excellence, to honor its many years of bringing the highest quality work to South Florida.

CHARACTERS

RACHEL STEIN - 16 year-old nihilistic Goth. Feels angry and orphaned since 9/11, as both of her parents have withdrawn into their own worlds.

SYLVIA STEIN - Her mother. 40s. Newly Evangelical, with a close, personal relationship to Jesus.

ARTHUR STEIN - Her father. 40s. Deeply depressed.

NELSON STEINBERG - Also 16 years old. Their new neighbor. Passionate about science, dresses as Elvis, loves Rachel.

JESUS and **STEPHEN HAWKING** - Played by the same actor.

SETTING

The Stein kitchen/den. We see the kitchen table, a glimpse of the appliance area to the rear, and a step down to a small den to the right.

Various other locations should be indicated with simple set pieces – a high school locker. The sign of a XXX movie theater. The table and chairs of a Starbucks.

TIME

Late September, 2003

For Alex, Charlie and David

(In the darkness, we hear an acoustic guitar. **NELSON** *is softly singing his ode to* **RACHEL***. A cantorial prayer blends in with, and then overtakes the guitar. It is then drowned out by an Evangelical choir. Each sound is beautiful and soulful, but as they begin competing for attention the sound becomes cacophonous and jarring. The music climaxes in one long discordant sound, which cuts out leaving only* **NELSON** *'s voice held in one long, pleading word. It has the wailing minor tones of a Hebraic prayer. RAAAACHHHEEEL. Lights come up on* **NELSON***. He is sixteen. He is dressed like Elvis. The 70's Elvis. He is playing guitar, singing a song he has written.)*

NELSON. *(singing)* Rachel. Rachel. Rachel Stein.

Harris High would be heaven, if you would be mine.

If I asked you to Borders, would you decline?

Rachel Stein.

(A pint sized milk carton is hurled onstage and hits **NELSON** *squarely on the side of the head. Far off laughter. He chuckles acknowledgement.)*

You guys!

(back to the song)

The first time I saw you was on the lunch line.

Cafeteria loud. Lunch two ninety-nine.

OFFSTAGE VOICE. Hey freak!

NELSON. We both chose the tuna. It seemed like a sign.

Rachel Stein.

OFFSTAGE VOICE. Asswipe!

NELSON. Ms. Holloway's class, the black board was thine.

You soared through equations like Albert Einstein.

OFFSTAGE VOICE. Yo. Jeff. Let's go kill the freak!

NELSON. Your mountainous math skills not short of Alpine.

Rachel...

(A general rallying war cry. A barrage of milk containers comes hurling at **NELSON***. Then the sounds of a stampede of Reeboks.)*

*(***NELSON*** finally takes the hint, gets up and dashes offstage.)*

OFFSTAGE VOICES. Kill the freak!!!!

(lights shift)

(A church bell chimes seven times. Lights up. Morning. The Stein kitchen. **ARTHUR** *sits in his pajamas, slumped across the kitchen table, asleep.)*

(Offstage we hear **SYLVIA***.)*

SYLVIA. Help! Oh no. Arthur! Help!

(The clatter of many books falling.)

Crap! Arthur, could you help me?

(huge crash)

Darn! Darn it!

(a beat)

*(***SYLVIA*** enters with an enormous stack of bibles, furious and disheveled.)*

Did you hear me? I was shouting for you.

ARTHUR. *(waking)* What? What time is it?

SYLVIA. The whole stack was coming down. It's a miracle I wasn't killed.

ARTHUR. I'm sorry. I didn't hear.

SYLVIA. Honestly.

(She goes back off and comes in with a poster of Jesus. It says, "Jesus Loves You" across the top.)

Did you spend the whole night out here again? Arthur?

ARTHUR. I must have dozed off.

SYLVIA. It's a beautiful day, praise God. You need to get showered and dressed.

(soto voce:)

You're starting to smell.

ARTHUR. I'm sorry.

SYLVIA. We're going door to door on West Lake this morning. You should join me.

(She goes back off and reenters with yet more bibles and a stack of brochures.)

And then this afternoon we're back in front of the triple X video store on Townsend. The first day we prayed there, twenty-two sinners went in. Last night it was less than ten. It's the miracle of prayer.

*(***JESUS***, the same ***JESUS*** as on the poster, enters from the other door, carrying a stack of bibles. Not sure where to put them. ***SYLVIA*** clears a spot.)*

Thank you, Jesus. Oh, I'll get the new youth group brochures. I can't wait to show you what I've done.

*(She rushes back out. ***JESUS*** follows. From offstage:)*

Did you make coffee? Arthur? Could you put up a pot?

(There is a knock on the door.)

Honey, could you get that?

*(***ARTHUR*** doesn't move. The door opens slightly.)*

NELSON. Hello?

*(***NELSON*** enters. Still in his Elvis attire. He has a guitar slung over his shoulder. His arm is now in a sling.)*

Hi. Is Rachel home?

SYLVIA. *(still offstage)* Who is it Hon?

ARTHUR. It's the king.

SYLVIA. The what?

ARTHUR. It's Elvis.

NELSON. Oh. No. I'm...Nelson Steinberg? We just moved in? Last month? Number 81?

ARTHUR. You're dressed like Elvis.

NELSON. Umm. Is Rachel here? I thought she lived here. I mean, I followed her home yesterday and I saw her come here.

ARTHUR. You followed her home?

NELSON. Yesterday. Well, yesterday and Wednesday. And Tuesday. And..

SYLVIA. *(entering with a stack of brochures, a knapsack and* **JESUS***)* Who was that at the…oh!

NELSON. Hi. I'm Nelson Steinberg? From 81?

ARTHUR. He's stalking Rachel.

SYLVIA. Hello.

NELSON. I live there? Across the street? Wow. I can't believe how much your place is like our place. They're like exactly alike.

ARTHUR. Condos.

NELSON. Except for the stuff inside. And our sink and refrigerator and stove and oven and counters and closet are on that side, and our table and chairs are on this side.

SYLVIA. You're the new people.

NELSON. One of them.

SYLVIA. Welcome! We prayed for you just last week!

NELSON. Thanks.

SYLVIA. I've been meaning to stop by with some baked goods but I'm just breathless with the ministry lately. The Rapture is coming, you know.

NELSON. It is?

SYLVIA. *(She and* **JESUS** *exchange a smile.)* That's what I hear!

NELSON. Great! What's the Rapture? It sounds so…

> *(***JESUS** *pulls out some flyers and* **SYLVIA** *hands them to* **NELSON***.)*

SYLVIA. Here!

NELSON. …intense. And passionate. The Rapture!

SYLVIA. This will tell you all about it. It's very important to welcome Jesus into your heart, Nathan, and truly repent, so that when End Days comes you'll be saved. Here, why don't you take one for your parents.

NELSON. Well, they're dead, actually.

SYLVIA. Oh…

NELSON. But I've got step-parents.

SYLVIA. Great! Do you have any friends you'd like to give some to?

NELSON. Oh, sure. I've got tons of friends.

(She gives him some more brochures.)

SYLVIA. *(to* JESUS*)* Look how well I'm doing today! And I haven't even left the house yet.

*(*JESUS *pats her back. Holds up another brochure.)*

Right! You know, Nathan, we have a very active youth group. Maybe you'd like to join them some time.

(an aside to JESUS*)*

Don't these look good? I changed the font.

NELSON. It looks great. Does Rachel belong?

SYLVIA. Well…

ARTHUR. No.

SYLVIA. Not yet.

NELSON. Umm…is she here?

SYLVIA. She must be getting dressed.

(calling up the stairs)

Rachel!

She must still be getting dressed. So…

NELSON. *(sitting at the table with* ARTHUR*)* That's okay. I can wait.

*(*SYLVIA *and* ARTHUR *and* JESUS *stare at him a moment.)*

SYLVIA. Well. All right then. You'll excuse me, Nathan. I need to get ready. I'm off to battle Satan!

NELSON. Nelson?

SYLVIA. *(confused)* Satan.

NELSON. No. My name, Ma'am. It's Nelson. Nelson Steinberg? It used to be Nelson Wallen, but then my step mom remarried and we changed our names and now it's Steinberg. Which is so great because I get to sit behind Rachel in homeroom. Stein. Steinberg?

SYLVIA. Oh.

NELSON. I also sit behind her in calculus. She's really great in math. Really great. Which is so wonderful for a girl. Not that girls are inherently poor in math, of course not, but, you know, sociological pressures make it uncommon for girls to excel in Math or Science. I bet she's great in science - wish I could sit behind her in science.

ARTHUR. Rachel's not allowed to take science any more.

NELSON. Wow. Too bad. Physics is amazing. They should start with physics in like kindergarten. Don't you think?

SYLVIA. Okay!

(*JESUS gives her a nod that they should go.*)

Well, I should be going!

NELSON. Kids would really pay attention in math if they had physics earlier.

(*JESUS gives* **SYLVIA** *a little tug on her sleeve.*)

SYLVIA. I still have to collate some flyers, so…

NELSON. I mean, it's like if they taught you to read before you could speak. You'd think, what are all these words, except you wouldn't think it in words, because you wouldn't know words yet.

(*JESUS points to his watch.*)

SYLVIA. I really do have to be getting ready. End Days isn't going to wait for me!

(*She and* **JESUS** *rush back out.*)

NELSON. Did I just talk too much?

ARTHUR. Maybe a little.

NELSON. Sometimes I do that. I'm supposed to look to see if anyone's interested but sometimes I forget to look, and sometimes even if I look it's hard to tell. People are really hard to read, don't you find?

ARTHUR. Yes.

NELSON. And then I get on a roll and it's hard for me to stop. I'm supposed to pretend to take an interest in the other person - ask questions so I don't monopolize the conversation, that's what they tell me.

ARTHUR. That seems sound.

NELSON. Thanks. So…

Tell me about yourself, Mr. S.

ARTHUR. What would you like to know?

NELSON. *(pulls a list out of his pocket and consults it)* Do you have any hobbies or special interests? That's usually a good icebreaker.

ARTHUR. Not really.

NELSON. *(goes back to the list)* What do you do for a living?

ARTHUR. I don't really do anything any more.

NELSON. Huh.

(list again)

Crazy weather we're having.

ARTHUR. I haven't been out for a while.

NELSON. Boy. This is tough. Any big plans for the day?

ARTHUR. I think I might just take a little nap.

NELSON. A nap! That's great. Were you up late last night with Rachel, conversing about her various interests or plans for the future?

ARTHUR. I just don't sleep.

NELSON. You don't?

ARTHUR. At night. And then, in the day it seems to be the only thing I can do.

NELSON. It sounds like you're off your cycle, sir.

ARTHUR. Maybe that's it.

NELSON. Or maybe you're clinically depressed. Have you seen a health care professional?

ARTHUR. Not lately.

NELSON. You shouldn't let that sort of thing go, Sir. Huge mood swings. Lack of sleep. How's your appetite?

ARTHUR. I don't know. I don't really eat.

NELSON. Sounds to me like you could use some help.

ARTHUR. I'll be okay.

NELSON. That's exactly what my father said, and then one morning we found him hanging from the basement ceiling pipes. None of us saw it coming. So you really can't take these things too lightly.

(*There is a long stunned silence.*)

That was inappropriate, wasn't it? Too much information. Didn't read the signs. Sorry about that.

ARTHUR. No, I appreciate your confidence.

NELSON. Really?

ARTHUR. Maybe I will make an appointment. Maybe a sleep clinic. Or something.

SYLVIA. (*reenters with* **JESUS**) Sleep clinic! You just need to do some good works.

Think about others instead of yourself and you'll sleep like a baby, am I right, Nelson? You need to welcome Jesus into your life.

NELSON. Or sometimes warm milk helps.

(**RACHEL** *enters. She is a scowling sixteen-year old Goth. White white skin, black hair, black clothes, black lips, black outlined eyes. She sees* **NELSON.** *Deeply suspicious.*)

RACHEL. What are you doing here?

NELSON. Rachel! Hi! Rachel.

(*quickly referencing his notes*)

I thought maybe since I was going that way maybe we could walk to school this morning. Together.

RACHEL. No thanks.

(*searching the cabinet*)

There's still no cereal.

SYLVIA. Honey, I thought you were going to go grocery shopping.

ARTHUR. I was so tired.

RACHEL. You haven't been out of those pajamas in three weeks.

(She finds a candy bar in a drawer and starts eating it.)

(under her breath)

You're starting to smell.

SYLVIA. Don't talk to your father like that.

ARTHUR. I'm sorry.

RACHEL. *(to* **NELSON***)* Shouldn't you be going to school?

SYLVIA. Your father needs our love and support, Rachel.

ARTHUR. I'll go shopping today.

SYLVIA. The ministry is praying for you, Arthur. I wish you would come with me. I know if you came and asked for Jesus' love and forgiveness, you would be healed.

*(***JESUS*** opens his arms to* **ARTHUR***.)*

ARTHUR. I'll go shopping. I really think I will.

*(***SYLVIA*** looks to* **JESUS***. He shrugs.)*

SYLVIA. Nelson. Have you accepted Jesus as your personal savior?

NELSON. No. But it sounds really interesting.

RACHEL. Okay. Time for school. Go Nelson.

SYLVIA. Have you read the good book?

RACHEL. Mom, just let him go.

NELSON. You mean the Bible?

RACHEL. You're going to be late.

SYLVIA. There's always time for the good news.

*(***JESUS*** hands her a Bible, which she adds to* **NELSON***'s pile of brochures.)*

Since I began a personal relationship with Jesus, my life is filled with joy and meaning, Nelson. I'm not afraid any more.

NELSON. That's so great.

SYLVIA. Maybe you'd like to come with us this Sunday. We're having a healing service.

NELSON. I'd love to! Wow. I've got Hebrew School at two but my morning is free.

ARTHUR. Hebrew school?

NELSON. My step-mom married Ben, so I'm converting and getting Bar Mitzvahed. It's a lot to learn on top of an eleventh grade curriculum but luckily I'm very bright. So, anyway, if your thing's in the morning that would be great.

SYLVIA. Eight a.m.

NELSON. Excellent! Thanks! Will you be going, Rachel?

RACHEL. No.

SYLVIA. Yes, she will.

NELSON. Great!

RACHEL. No.

SYLVIA. She'll be going and Arthur will be going and now you'll be going!

ARTHUR. I think I'm free, but...

RACHEL. I'm not. Now go to school, Nelson.

SYLVIA. Honey, this week it's nonnegotiable.

RACHEL. I'm not going to sit through that bullshit.

SYLVIA. Rachel! Don't use that language.

RACHEL. "Religion is all bullshit." Remember?

SYLVIA. *(to* JESUS, *who is shocked)* I never said...

RACHEL. Whenever Grandma and Grandpa asked to bring me to Shul...

SYLVIA. Honey – Grandma and Grandpa were Ultra Orthodox.

RACHEL. So?

SYLVIA. So that was a whole other thing. That was very extreme.

RACHEL. *(motions to the Bibles and signs) That* was extreme? Are you fucking kidding me?

SYLVIA. Rachel! Your grandmother shaved her head and wore a wig. All right? And your grandfather – if he were alive, he wouldn't even touch you now. Once I turned twelve he wouldn't touch me because I might be "unclean."

(At this, **JESUS** *backs out of the room.)*

RACHEL. They were my grandparents. They wanted me to come with them.

SYLVIA. The whole service was in Hebrew. You wouldn't have understood a word of it.

RACHEL. Whose fault is that?

SYLVIA. Where is this coming from? You didn't want to go. I let you choose and you chose not to.

ARTHUR. *(under this, to himself)* I'm so tired.

RACHEL. I was five years old! You said it was bullshit, what do you think I'd say?

SYLVIA. All right. Fine. You want to go to Shul –

RACHEL. *(overlapping)* I'm not saying that's what I want.

SYLVIA. The women sit behind a curtain so the men won't be distracted from their holy thoughts…

RACHEL. You don't even listen to what I want.

SYLVIA. I'll drop you off there on Saturday! Or no. You want to be Orthodox – you can walk.

NELSON. You could come with me! We're reform so – hey! We could even sit together!

RACHEL. I don't want any of it. *I* still think it's bullshit. I just don't understand what *you* want any more.

SYLVIA. Come with me to Blessed Name. Come and you'll understand.

RACHEL. It's like you shut off part of your brain.

SYLVIA. I'm happy.

RACHEL. I hate happy.

SYLVIA. Rachel…

RACHEL. You told me there was no God. That when we died, we were dead and that sucked but deal with it.

SYLVIA. *(reaching for her)* But that's terrible, honey. I'm sorry I told you that.

*(**JESUS** drifts back into the room and stands beside* **SYLVIA***.)*

RACHEL. *(pulling away, very upset)* You told me to think for myself. Remember? I mean, we read Kafka together when everyone else was reading *Little Women*. We read Camus. I don't understand what happened.

(**JESUS** *puts his hand on* **SYLVIA**'s *shoulder.*)

SYLVIA. Look. Honey. If you came to Blessed Name...

RACHEL. No.

SYLVIA. I'm not doing this to punish you. I love you.

RACHEL. *(suddenly furious)* Then buy some fucking groceries!

SYLVIA. Rachel!

RACHEL. Stop shoving all this crap down my throat! Stop parading all over town with your nutty signs. Stop embarrassing me.

SYLVIA. I'm not trying to embarrass you. I'm trying to save you.

RACHEL. Yeah. I'll pass, thanks.

SYLVIA. I'm terrified for you, Rachel. You're going to be left behind. When the Rapture comes...

RACHEL. Then I'll stay behind! I'll take frogs and leeches and blood in the streets over all your holier than thou crap.

SYLVIA. That's it! Go to your room!

RACHEL. I have school.

SYLVIA. You're not going to school today. Get upstairs.

RACHEL. Jesus wants me to be a truant now?

SYLVIA. Listen, you. Do not talk to me like that. I'm your mother. If I decide to home school you...

RACHEL. Home school me?

SYLVIA. ...then you don't go to public school any more.

RACHEL. You're never home!

SYLVIA. *(overlapping)* If I send you to religious school, you go to religious school. If I send you to reform school, you go to reform school.

(**JESUS** *tries to calm* **SYLVIA** *down. She shrugs him off* *and he quickly walks offstage.)*

RACHEL. *(over* **SYLVIA***)* Reform school? You're nuts. You've totally lost your mind.

SYLVIA. You're a minor. You do what I say. And you are going to church Sunday morning. If I have to drag you by the hair I'll do it.

RACHEL. Gee, that doesn't sound very Christian.

SYLVIA. *(completely frustrated and furious)* Look! Look, you people! I am trying to do something here. I am trying to save this family! I have found something…I have finally found something that has given me hope and joy and peace. I'm happy. Since Jesus came into my life, I am finally happy! And you people are not going to ruin this for me. You hear? Rachel? Arthur? You're both coming with me on Sunday and you are going to listen to the Good Word, and you are going to open your hearts and let Jesus save you!

(There is a pause. We hear the squeal of bus brakes.)

RACHEL. There's the bus! See ya!

(She grabs her books and races out the door.)

NELSON. Wait! Rachel, I thought maybe…

(But she's gone.)

(Pause. **SYLVIA** *notices that* **JESUS** *is gone. Frightened.)*

SYLVIA. Jesus?

(He comes back into the room.)

Oh, God.

(collecting herself)

Well, I really should get going too.

*(***JESUS** *hands her her backpack.)*

Thank you, Jesus. All right then.

(chipper again)

You get dressed and go shopping now, Arthur! I'll see you Sunday, Nelson. Have a blessed day!

(She takes her backpack and signs and she and **JESUS** *leave.* **NELSON** *and* **ARTHUR** *sit in silence for a moment.)*

NELSON. Wow. Rachel really doesn't seem to like me.

ARTHUR. She doesn't seem to like me either.

(They both sit glumly for a moment.)

NELSON. Guess I should head out too then.

ARTHUR. Do you have to?

NELSON. Well, I've got school.

ARTHUR. Right.

NELSON. So…

ARTHUR. You could skip it.

NELSON. What?

ARTHUR. If you feel like. We could play cards or something. You ever play gin, Nelson?

NELSON. I don't think so.

ARTHUR. I could teach you. It's not hard.

NELSON. Well, we've got calculus.

ARTHUR. Oh.

NELSON. First period.

ARTHUR. Oh. Okay.

NELSON. Yeah.

(pause)

I really would like to learn, though. I mean, I've often thought that. That I'd like to learn cards.

*(***ARTHUR** *doesn't respond.)*

So…

(pause)

Hey, what if I came after school? How would that be?

ARTHUR. Okay.

NELSON. Great! I'll come back after school. And we could play some card games.

ARTHUR. Okay.

*(***NELSON** *starts to leave. Turns back.)*

NELSON. Do you think you might go shopping today? Rachel seemed kind of mad about that.

ARTHUR. I guess.

NELSON. I think you should.

ARTHUR. I don't know, Nelson. It all seems exhausting lately.

NELSON. What?

ARTHUR. All of it. Sleeping and getting up and washing and eating and using the john.

NELSON. Huh.

ARTHUR. We do it all every day and then…what? We do it all again and again and again and again. And then… eventually we don't do it any more.

NELSON. I'll come after school, okay?

ARTHUR. Okay.

NELSON. You'll go shopping. And then I'll come after school.

ARTHUR. Okay.

(Light shift. Cafeteria sounds. **RACHEL** *sits at a long, empty table, reading a textbook.)*

*(***NELSON*** heads toward her, struggling to hold his tray while maneuvering around the sling and the guitar. There is now a large bandage across the bridge of his nose.)*

NELSON. Rachel! Hi! Rachel. Mind if I join you?

RACHEL. *(refusing to look up)* Yes.

NELSON. Oh.

(He looks around blankly.)

RACHEL. There's an empty table over there.

NELSON. Okay.

(But he just stands there, silent for a moment. Then:)

You were so amazing this morning. At the blackboard. Had you worked out that equation before? Because you wrote it out so fast. It's like you were channeling it or…something…

(RACHEL finally looks up at him.)

RACHEL. What happened to your nose?

NELSON. This? Oh, I was just horsing around with some of the guys.

RACHEL. If you'd stop dressing like that, they might stop beating you up.

NELSON. No, no. We were just roughhousing. It was all in fun.

A VOICE FROM OFFSTAGE. Hey freak!

(An empty milk carton comes flying through the air and clocks NELSON in the head. Laughter.)

NELSON. *(laughingly, to them)* You guys!

Anyway, Nurse Liz is real nice. Stopped the bleeding in about two seconds. Patched me right up.

RACHEL. Whatever.

(She goes back to her book.)

NELSON. I was saying to your dad, it's too bad you're not taking physics. With your calculus, you'd be a natural.

RACHEL. Yeah. Look, don't come by my house any more, okay? And don't tell anybody about…anything at my house. Okay?

NELSON. You can count on me, Rachel. What happens between us, stays between us.

RACHEL. Great.

(She goes back to her book. Barely acknowledges him through the following.)

NELSON. *(Trying to consult some notes, while balancing his tray.)* I can't believe how alike our houses are.

RACHEL. Uh huh.

NELSON. Have you lived there long?

RACHEL. No.

NELSON. Where are you from?

RACHEL. New York.

NELSON. New York City? Wow. You're from New York City. How great is that?

RACHEL. Great.

NELSON. Why did you move?

RACHEL. My dad lost his job.

NELSON. Oh. How did he…

RACHEL. It blew up when a plane flew into it.

NELSON. A plane…Wow. Was he okay?

RACHEL. Oh yeah. He's great.

*(Another milk carton beans **NELSON** in the head. Laughter offstage.)*

NELSON. *(To offstage boys.)* Hey! You've got quite an arm!

(Another carton comes flying in.)

RACHEL. *(Shouting offstage.)* Stop it you freakin' goons!

(more laughter offstage)

(to **NELSON**) Sit. Would you just sit for Christ's sakes.

NELSON. Gee. Thanks.

(He eagerly sits down and starts eating his macaroni and cheese.)

They've got very good macaroni and cheese here. Much better than my last school. Less gooey.

RACHEL. I'd really like to just read, okay?

NELSON. Yeah? Me too. I love to read. Did you ever read this?

(He holds up his book. "A Brief History of Time.")

RACHEL. What is it?

NELSON. It's only the greatest book ever written.

RACHEL. What *is* it?

NELSON. Stephen Hawking explains pretty much everything in the universe.

RACHEL. Does he explain why you're dressed like that?

NELSON. No, you know, like all the great scientific theories from Aristotle and Ptolemy pretty much up until now.

RACHEL. Oh.

NELSON. You would love it.

RACHEL. I don't think so.

NELSON. No, you would – I mean, it all comes down to math. Unification. To have a mathematical equation that integrates Einstein's general relativity with quantum mechanics. An equation that encompasses everything.

RACHEL. And then what?

NELSON. And then we know how it all works.

RACHEL. And then what?

NELSON. And then we can figure out how it all started.

RACHEL. And then what?

NELSON. Ummm. And then we know.

(RACHEL *goes back to her book.*)

He's so amazing. Stephen Hawking. He's got A.L.S. – they told him he'd die when he was like twenty, and he's lived more than forty years past that and he rides around in a motorized wheelchair and he talks through a computer. It's like the greatest brain on the planet riding around on this chair. You want to borrow it?

RACHEL. No thanks.

NELSON. It's okay. I've got my name in the cover.

RACHEL. No.

NELSON. It's really easy. I mean, it's written in a way that anyone can understand.

(*pause*)

Come on. Take it. And then you can tell me what you think.

(*She takes the book.*)

Great! Wow! This is so great!

RACHEL. I probably won't read it.

NELSON. But you might.

RACHEL. I might.

NELSON. And then we could talk about it. Oh my God. That would be just about the greatest thing ever.

(RACHEL *looks at him for a long moment.*)

RACHEL. You should stop wearing that outfit.

NELSON. That's okay.

RACHEL. They won't stop beating on you till you stop.

NELSON. I'm used to it.

RACHEL. But why get used to it? Why not just be normal?

NELSON. Why do you wear that outfit?

RACHEL. So people will leave me alone.

NELSON. Oh.

RACHEL. Clearly it's not working.

NELSON. Some people think he's like a savior or something. Elvis. That he didn't really die, or that he'll rise again.

RACHEL. They're nuts.

NELSON. Maybe. My mom loved him. She got me an Elvis outfit for Halloween when I was five and I would never take it off.

RACHEL. That was probably cute. When you were five.

NELSON. Yeah. So, I just kept on wearing it. Everywhere. Even to my Mom's funeral I wore it. My dad finally threw it away and I wouldn't get dressed. Went to kindergarten in my underwear.

RACHEL. You're kidding.

NELSON. Nope. So eventually he got me a new one. I find it really comforting. We've got the same birthday. Elvis and I. January 8th. And guess who else has it?

RACHEL. Who?

NELSON. Guess.

RACHEL. No.

NELSON. Come on. Somebody amazing.

RACHEL. Just tell me for Christ sakes.

NELSON. Stephen Hawking! The guy I was just telling you about! The book guy.

RACHEL. So?

NELSON. Isn't that cool?

RACHEL. Maybe you should dress like him.

NELSON. It's okay. They always beat me up the first month or so. But it gets old after a while. I expect it'll stop soon.

*(A barrage of milk containers starts hammering at them.
Laughter offstage.)*

RACHEL. *(Snapping from 1 to 10 in about a second. Picks up the
milk containers and starts pummeling them back.)* Leave us
alone you freakin' assholes!

NELSON. Wow. You've got great aim!

RACHEL. Friggin' Neanderthals!

*(**NELSON** picks up a container with his good arm and
hurls it back, weakly.)*

NELSON. Friggin' Neanderthals!

(He grins, delighted.)

*(Light shift. **SYLVIA** is on a folding chair in front of the
XXX video store. She is having a little chat with someone
off stage. There is an empty folding chair beside her.)*

SYLVIA. So finally I say, *(flirting)* "Well, I would love it if you
came with me, Mr. Jenks. We could sit together."
And – boom. You know? But I thought, hey, if we can
just get him there.

*(**JESUS** enters with two paper cups of hot coffee and joins
SYLVIA in the other folding chair.)*

SYLVIA. Thank you, Jesus.

JESUS. You're welcome, Sylvia.

SYLVIA. *(with growing passion and fury)* It's so frustrating. I
wanted to say, "Mr. Jenks, the world is a horrible, dan-
gerous, terrifying place. At any moment you could
be raped, or knifed or gunned down. Some tsunami
could wipe out your village, or you could get mad cow
disease, or a meteor could hit, or a bus could plow into
you, or you could be poisoned by anthrax, or some
crazy foreign fanatic could try to blow you up."

*(**JESUS** looks disapproving)*

But, of course you can't say that. Can you?

JESUS. No.

(They both take a sip.)

SYLVIA. This is very good coffee.

But, I mean, hello! Here you are offering him eternal life and safety, off this Earth, in Heaven, where nobody who would harm him could even get in.

JESUS. *(putting a pink packet into his coffee)* Sweetener?

SYLVIA. I'm good, thanks. I know you said, "blessed are the poor in spirit." Remember when you said that? In Matthew?

JESUS. Right.

SYLVIA. But, enough already. Get some spirit. Get on board. Anyway, he loved being at the mission so much, he said he's going to come every week. So, it all worked out. And can you imagine, we nearly lost him to the Unitarians.

JESUS. Sylvia!

SYLVIA. Sorry.

(**JESUS** *laughs.*)

JESUS. Well. No, you're right.

(**SYLVIA** *laughs.*)

SYLVIA. Oh Jesus! I just love you so much!

JESUS. I love you too, Sylvia.

SYLVIA. You really saved a wretch like me, you know? I wish everyone felt what I feel! I wish I could talk about you to every single person on earth.

JESUS. You're off to a good start, Sylvia.

SYLVIA. Thanks.

(They each take a sip.)

This is nice. Here.

JESUS. Yes.

SYLVIA. Praise God. Before you came into my life, there's no way in heck I would be out here sipping coffee in the broad daylight where any drive-by shooter could take me out. And now – let 'em try. Death is just a gateway to a lifetime with you.

JESUS. Amen.

SYLVIA. How do I get through to Rachel and Arthur, Jesus? I really lost my mind this morning, didn't I? Reform school? Crazy.

JESUS. You just want the best for them. You're a good person, Sylvia.

SYLVIA. Am I?

JESUS. You're a good person. And you're doing good in the world.

SYLVIA. Thank you, Jesus. It means so much to me that you think so.

JESUS. I do.

SYLVIA. Well, they're coming Sunday. Maybe they'll be moved by the spirit.

JESUS. I'll do what I can.

SYLVIA. Oh look! Here come some sinners!

JESUS. Time to pray.

(They bow their heads.)

*(Light shift. **RACHEL** is sitting somewhere outside the school, rolling a joint. She lights up, leans back, and begins reading "A Brief History of Time.")*

*(A church bell chimes four times. Lights up on **ARTHUR**. He is still at the kitchen table, but is now lying across it, asleep.)*

(There is a knock at the door.)

NELSON. *(offstage)* Mr. S.?

(Arthur doesn't waken.)

*(**NELSON** knocks again, then enters, now on crutches. His nose is still bandaged and his arm still in a sling.)*

Mr. S.?

*(He sees **ARTHUR** slumped over the table. Rushes to him, shakes him.)*

Oh no! Mr. S.! Mr. S.!

*(**ARTHUR** rouses with a start.)*

ARTHUR. What? What time is it?

NELSON. Don't scare me like that, Mr. S. I thought you'd done something drastic.

ARTHUR. Is school over?

NELSON. For an hour. I waited outside to follow Rachel home, but she never came. You're still in your pajamas.

ARTHUR. Oh. Yeah.

NELSON. I guess you didn't go shopping, huh?

ARTHUR. I guess not. Do you want to play gin?

NELSON. Let's go get some groceries. Do you have a car?

ARTHUR. Not any more.

NELSON. Well, we'll walk. It'll be good for us, right? And cereal doesn't weigh too much.

ARTHUR. I don't know, Nelson. I'm kind of tired.

NELSON. Where are your clothes?

ARTHUR. I'll go tomorrow. Definitely.

NELSON. Go get dressed.

ARTHUR. I haven't been outside in a while, Nelson.

NELSON. It'll be fun.

ARTHUR. A long while.

NELSON. It'll be an adventure.

(*Lights shift.* **RACHEL** *is running to her locker at school. The hallway is dimly lit and empty. She madly starts entering her combination code. The lock doesn't budge. She tries it again, more frantic. Nothing. She begins banging on the locker and kicking it. She completely loses it and kicks and pounds on the locker hysterically. Crumples to the foot of the locker, defeated and spent.*)

(**STEPHEN HAWKING** *appears from behind the locker. He is in his motorized wheelchair with its electronic speaking device. His voice is the unearthly robotic monotone of the computer.*)

STEPHEN HAWKING. Maybe you should get the janitor.

(**RACHEL** *stares at him, speechless.*)

Or you could just kick it some more. That seems productive.

RACHEL. *(stunned)* Oh my God. I was just reading your book.

STEPHEN. Did you buy it?

RACHEL. No, it's Nelson's copy.

STEPHEN. You should buy it. I like it when people buy it.

RACHEL. How did you get here?

STEPHEN. Chair.

RACHEL. Oh my God. I'm cracking up. I'm my mother. I'm a nut like my mother.

STEPHEN. You seem to be having a problem with your locker.

RACHEL. Oh my God. Oh my God.

STEPHEN. And you're an atheist of convenience. Very sensible.

RACHEL. Did you come here...did you...did you travel through a wormhole?

STEPHEN. You haven't read the papers?

RACHEL. Huh?

STEPHEN. I was wrong about the wormholes. There's no surviving them.

RACHEL. Wow.

STEPHEN. Bummer, right?

RACHEL. How are you here? Am I crazy? I'm losing my mind, aren't I?

STEPHEN. This is your mind on drugs.

RACHEL. I was reading. I lost track of time.

STEPHEN. Space and time not only affect but are also affected by everything that happens in the universe. Think about it.

RACHEL. They're going to lock down the school. I can't get my books. I can't open my locker. I don't know what to do.

STEPHEN. 32-7-46.

RACHEL. Huh?

STEPHEN. Your locker.

RACHEL. 32-7-46!

*(She jumps up and tries the combination. The locker opens. She turns around. **STEPHEN HAWKING** is gone.)*

*(Light shift. **NELSON** and **ARTHUR** standing in the cereal aisle at Shoprite.)*

NELSON. Crunchy? Flaky?

ARTHUR. I don't know.

NELSON. Does she like frosted or plain?

ARTHUR. I don't know.

NELSON. Chex? Raisin Bran? Total?

ARTHUR. I don't know, Nelson.

(They move a few inches.)

NELSON. Wow. There sure are a lot of cereals. Okay. Try to picture her sitting down to breakfast.

ARTHUR. I can't. I can't picture her at all.

NELSON. She has an empty bowl in front of her.

ARTHUR. No.

NELSON. A spoon. A napkin.

ARTHUR. I can't do this, Nelson. This is too hard.

NELSON. She reaches out. She picks up a box. She opens it and pours it into her bowl...What color is the box?!

*(Pause. **ARTHUR** crumbles.)*

ARTHUR. I don't know. I never noticed what color box her cereal was in. I never noticed that she ate cereal. I was out of the house before she got up. I came home at 9. I don't know what she ate for dinner. I don't know what she packed for lunch.

NELSON. She buys actually.

ARTHUR. I don't know. I don't know her. Let's go. Please. Let's go home.

NELSON. You could get to know her now. It'll be fun. We could both get to know her.

ARTHUR. She doesn't want me to know her.

NELSON. That's okay. She doesn't want me to know her either. You just have to be persistent.

ARTHUR. She hates me.

NELSON. No.

ARTHUR. I don't blame her.

NELSON. She doesn't hate you.

ARTHUR. I used to be a Senior Vice President. I used to wear a suit and tie. Now I can't even get dressed.

NELSON. You are dressed.

ARTHUR. I used to tell sixty-five people what to do. All those people. All gone.

NELSON. How about Rice Crispies?

ARTHUR. If I hadn't run into that guy in the stairwell. Some guy with a flashlight. I don't know who that guy was. I'll never know.

NELSON. Or maybe Corn Flakes.

ARTHUR. I'd be gone too. I should be gone too.

NELSON. I bet she likes Cheerios. Everyone likes Cheerios.

ARTHUR. Sixty-five people. Now I can't even get dressed.

NELSON. You are dressed, Mr. S.

(*pause*)

Hey, we'll get one of everything! It'll be great. We'll get one of every cereal. And we'll all eat breakfast together. Every day.

ARTHUR. I don't eat.

NELSON. Now you'll eat. We'll eat cereal.

(*Light shift. We hear a rendition of "Amazing Grace" as the church bell chimes ten times.*)

(*Lights up on the Stein kitchen. We hear the church-goers* SYLVIA, JESUS, ARTHUR, RACHEL *and* NELSON *returning. As they enter:*)

SYLVIA. Never. I mean, I've only been worshipping for three months but I've never seen a triple miracle, praise God. And on your first time.

NELSON. (*modestly*) I just felt…I mean, the music was so beautiful.

(As we see NELSON, the bandage is off his nose. SYLVIA is carrying his sling and his crutches.)

SYLVIA. You let Jesus into your heart, and he made you whole. Reverend Peter was beside himself. I only wish I'd been able to fill every pew in the church to witness it.

(RACHEL goes to the cabinet and takes down some Life cereal. She pours it into a bowl. ARTHUR, exhausted, goes to his place at the table and slumps down, more depressed than ever.)

It meant so much to me that you three came today. Thank you. Thank you Jesus.

RACHEL. *(looking in the refrigerator)* I should have prayed for milk.

NELSON. Oh no! We forgot milk!

(RACHEL begins eating her cereal dry.)

SYLVIA. While we're all so moved by the spirit, shall we make a whole day of it? I'm on my way to the women's shelter. We're ministering to the poor and offering hot lunches.

(JESUS reaches under the counter and brings out a huge soup tureen.)

RACHEL. Could you bring me back some food?

SYLVIA. Rachel! Why don't you come? You won't believe the feeling you get helping someone less fortunate.

RACHEL. I'm hungry.

SYLVIA. Arthur?

ARTHUR. I'm a little tired.

NELSON. Gosh, I'd love to. It sounds very life affirming, but I've got to go over my Torah portion before my private with Mr. Levine. He's really going at quite a clip.

SYLVIA. Your Torah portion?

NELSON. Two kids are turning thirteen next month so we might do a triple Bar Mitzvah. But Rabbi Baumbach says I really have to pick up the pace.

SYLVIA. *(to* **NELSON***)* I just thought...I mean, you just had this life changing experience...

NELSON. I did. Absolutely.

SYLVIA. Oh.

(She takes the soup tureen from **JESUS.***)*

Thank you, Jesus. So, will you be coming next Sunday? To Blessed Name?

NELSON. Definitely. I wouldn't miss it.

ARTHUR. Think I might take a little nap.

(He exits.)

*(***JESUS** *gives* **SYLVIA** *a little pat on the shoulder and she is strengthened by it.)*

SYLVIA. All right then. We'll all go together again! Wonderful. Have a blessed afternoon everyone!

RACHEL. Ta.

*(***SYLVIA** *and* **JESUS** *leave.)*

NELSON. So...How about that? What a morning, right?

*(***RACHEL** *wads up a brochure and throws it at him. It beans him in the head.)*

NELSON. Oops!

RACHEL. Catch!

(She throws another wad, which he swats at with his left hand.)

NELSON. What are you doing, Rachel?

RACHEL. Catch, damn it!

(She throws. He tries to catch with his right arm but it hurts.)

NELSON. Ow!

RACHEL. "I'm healed! Thank you Jesus! I can see!"

NELSON. I didn't say that.

RACHEL. Freakin' phony. Let me see you hop on one leg.

(He does.)

The sprained leg, stupid.

(He tries but it is clearly painful.)

NELSON. Well, maybe I'm not completely healed. But I'm feeling considerably better.

RACHEL. Yeah. It's a miracle.

(She returns to her dry cereal.)

NELSON. Didn't you love it there, Rachel? The music was so stirring, and Reverend Peter had such a deep booming voice and everyone was so nice. I really felt part of something big, didn't you?

RACHEL. God whore.

NELSON. What?

RACHEL. You have to pick, don't you get that? You can't be Jewish on Saturday and Evangelical on Sunday, just to cover all your bases.

NELSON. But I like them both.

RACHEL. You're not supposed to "like" them. And they're completely contradictory.

NELSON. Everything's contradictory. It's like Quantum Field Theory.

RACHEL. No it's not.

NELSON. It is. If you ask, "Is light a particle or a wave?" Well, actually, it can be both. I mean, if you ask a particle-like question, you get a particle-like answer, and if you ask a wave-like question, you get a wave-like answer. You just can't ask both questions at the same time.

RACHEL. Is this what you do every time you move?

NELSON. What?

RACHEL. You follow some girl home. Feed her astrophysics. Join her mother's freak-show church.

NELSON. I just…I like you, Rachel.

RACHEL. You have no reason to like me.

NELSON. Maybe it's pheromones.

RACHEL. Huh?

NELSON. Maybe you're giving off an indiscernible smell that I can't consciously recognize but that my body chemically responds to.

RACHEL. Don't smell me then, okay!? Don't smell me. Don't like me. And don't come around here pumping up my mother any more. She's fucking lost her mind and I don't need you here feeding her sick fantasies.

NELSON. I think your mom just loves you. My mom was like that. She wants you to be safe.

RACHEL. My mother has been inculcated into a cult.

NELSON. Maybe. Or maybe she's asking a wave-like question and you're asking a particle-like question.

RACHEL. That is such bullshit! How do you shove all this science down my throat and then act like you're healed. You genuinely think you were healed by God today?

NELSON. Probably not.

RACHEL. Probably not.

NELSON. But the idea of it made me happy. I would have liked there to be a miracle.

RACHEL. See, I like REALITY! Well, I don't like it. But everything else pisses me off!

NELSON. I'm sorry, Rachel. I wish I could stop pissing you off. I wish I could say the right thing. I never can say the right thing, and I want so much to say the right thing to you.

(Long pause while **RACHEL** *considers this.)*

RACHEL. I read your book.

NELSON. The Stephen Hawking? You read the Stephen Hawking? Oh my gosh. Why didn't you tell me?

RACHEL. You were too busy speaking in tongues.

NELSON. What did you think? Did you like it?

(Pause. Sigh.)

RACHEL. Yeah. I liked it.

NELSON. Oh my Gosh. You liked it. Wow. This is like the greatest day of my life.

RACHEL. But it's not about all that miracle crap. It's about figuring out…

NELSON. *(over this)* This is so great.! You liked it. I knew…I just knew you would. Oh my gosh. There are so many things I want you to read. Brian Green, Ta-Pei Cheng, Simon Signh.

(searching through his backpack)

I've got articles…Videos…Do you know about the LHC?

RACHEL. The what?

NELSON. The Large Hadron Collider. Oh my gosh, Rachel. You're going to love this. They're building this enormous machine at CERN, outside Geneva, Switzerland. It's this incredibly long tunnel where they'll smash together particles with such speed and energy…they might be able to create conditions that were present in the universe a billionth of a second after the Big Bang. Oh my gosh.

(back to searching through his backpack)

I've got this article. You're going to love this. Where did I…

RACHEL. Wait. They might be able to prove the Big Bang?

NELSON. They might be able to replicate it.

RACHEL. And prove it wasn't God?

NELSON. Well, nobody knows that. But the science is so thrilling. I want to tell you so much! I've got so much…Soon…like in the next few years we're going to be able to observe so many things that were once only wild concepts.

RACHEL. Yeah?

NELSON. Wonderful things. Unimaginable things. Technology is catching up with theory. Fast. Really, really fast. I mean, this is the greatest time to be alive.

RACHEL. *(A beat. Amazed.)* You really believe that, don't you?

NELSON. I do. Absolutely. We're so lucky. Oh, Rachel. I'm so happy you read the book. I'm so happy.

*(**RACHEL** considers him. She grabs his face, a bit violently. He recoils, afraid he's going to get his nose broken again. She pulls him back in and kisses him fast, awkwardly.)*

NELSON. *(dazed)* What was that?

RACHEL. *(baffled herself)* I don't know. An experiment.

NELSON. You kissed me. Right?

RACHEL. Tell me more. The Large…

NELSON. Uhh…Hadron Collider. Yeah.

(She kisses him again.)

NELSON. Yeah.

Yeah. They might be able to collide protons at such
high speeds? They'll be broken down so small, they
might be able to pinpoint the smallest fragments of
the universe. They might be able to prove that all of
matter, each of us, is made up of strings. That we're all
strings, vibrating like an infinitely small orchestra.

(She kisses him again.)

You kissed me three times. What does it mean?

RACHEL. I don't know.

NELSON. Does it mean you like me?

RACHEL. I don't know.

(She kisses him again.)

Maybe.

NELSON. Probably?

RACHEL. Maybe.

(She kisses him again.)

Tell me more.

*(Lights shift. A bit later. NELSON is sitting at the kitchen
table, playing a tape of his Torah portion and staring off
into space. RACHEL has left. He reaches the end of the
tape and hits rewind.)*

(ARTHUR enters in his pajamas.)

ARTHUR. What time is it?

NELSON. Mr. S.! I'm so glad you're awake. Something unbelievable has happened.

ARTHUR. What was that singing? I thought I was dead.

NELSON. Mr. S., Rachel kissed me.

ARTHUR. Who?

NELSON. Your daughter, Rachel Stein.

ARTHUR. She kissed you?

NELSON. Seven times. And then she left. What does it mean?

ARTHUR. Was she armed?

NELSON. No.

ARTHUR. Did she look angry?

NELSON. Not really.

ARTHUR. I wonder what it means.

NELSON. You don't know?

ARTHUR. Did she say anything?

NELSON. She said it was an experiment.

ARTHUR. Maybe it really is the end of days.

NELSON. Yeah?

ARTHUR. I'm feeling a little light headed.

NELSON. When's the last time you ate?

ARTHUR. Yesterday, I think. What's today?

NELSON. Sunday.

ARTHUR. Maybe it was Friday.

NELSON. I think you better eat something.

ARTHUR. Weren't you practicing your Torah portion? It sounded good.

NELSON. Well, that was the tape.

ARTHUR. Let me hear you.

NELSON. I think you should eat something.

ARTHUR. After. I'll eat something after.

NELSON. You promise?

ARTHUR. Yes. Sing.

NELSON. *(sings, like Elvis)* Vayomer Elohim le-Noach ket kol-basar
ba lefanay ki-male'al ha'arets chamas

ARTHUR. It's good.

NELSON. Is it right?

ARTHUR. You've got a nice voice. What is it?

NELSON. Noah. Genesis. How's my pronunciation? Can you help me?

ARTHUR. Let me have a look.

NELSON. *(handing* ARTHUR *his bible)* Here's where it starts. And here's the transliteration. And I've got the translations back here.

*(*ARTHUR *tries to read it.)*

Here, sir. Here it is. "And God said to Noah…"

ARTHUR. I need my glasses.

NELSON. Where are they?

ARTHUR. I'm not sure.

NELSON. When did you use them last?

ARTHUR. It could have been…a year.

(The truth of this hits him.)

Or…more. More.

NELSON. You haven't read anything in a year, Mr. S.?

*(*ARTHUR *doesn't answer.)*

I could look for them.

*(*ARTHUR *just sits in thought.)*

It's okay, sir.

Hey, I'll read it to you. I'll read what it means, and then you can help me with the Hebrew. Okay?

Here. "And God said to Noah, 'The end of all flesh has come before Me. The world is filled with man's crime. I will therefore destroy them with the earth.'"

*(*ARTHUR *sits silent.)*

Pretty wrathful stuff, right, sir?

Both Bibles are like that. It wasn't what I expected. I guess it's to scare us into being good, right? Unless you take it literally like Mrs. S. and then God just said things like that because he was a really angry guy.

ARTHUR. I don't know, Nelson.

NELSON. Anyway, I guess it doesn't really matter so much, right? What it means. For now. Mostly I just need it to sound right.

ARTHUR. I don't think I ever thought too much about what it means.

NELSON. Yeah, well…

ARTHUR. All those years of Hebrew school. I wonder why I never thought about what it means.

NELSON. Mostly they want the Hebrew to be right. So, could you sing it for me?

ARTHUR. Me? No, no, my voice is shot.

NELSON. But if you know how to say it…

(pause)

ARTHUR. In the drawer. There should be a magnifying glass. There.

*(**NELSON** gets it for him.)*

Good. Let's see.

(sings)

Vayomer Elohim le-Noach ket kol-basar
ba lefanay ki-male'al ha'arets…

NELSON. Wow. That was *so* authentic. I mean, really. That was really really great.

ARTHUR. Yeah?

NELSON. You sound just like Cantor Epstein.

ARTHUR. No.

NELSON. Really.

ARTHUR. *(very flattered)* Well. I used to be okay. A million years ago.

NELSON. No way. You're like the real deal, sir.

ARTHUR. I led the whole thing, you know. My Bar Mitzvah.

NELSON. You led the whole service?

ARTHUR. Soup to nuts.

NELSON. That's very impressive, Sir.

ARTHUR. Temple Sholom. I still have the pen my Grandpa Al gave me.

(He feels for it in his pocket, then realizes.)

Pajamas.

NELSON. I hope you'll come. To mine, I mean. Bar Mitzvah.

ARTHUR. When is it?

NELSON. It should be in October, but…

ARTHUR. It doesn't matter, Nelson. Of course I'm going to come.

NELSON. Excellent, sir!

ARTHUR. We better get working. I want you to do me proud. Sing that first line again.

NELSON. *(now trying to sound like* **ARTHUR**, *rather than Elvis)*
Vayomer Elohim le-Noach ket kol-basar
ba lefanay ki-male'al ha'arets

(His pronunciation is bad, but his voice is clear and beautiful.)

ARTHUR. *(very moved)* That's beautiful.

NELSON. I know I need to listen to the tape more.

ARTHUR. It's beautiful. All right. Let's get to work. Vayom*er*, not Vayom*ar*. You see?

NELSON. Vayomer.

ARTHUR. Good. Vayomer Elhim le-Noach kets kol-basar – not kol-baser, okay?

NELSON. Kol basar. Good. That's good, sir. Very good.
Vayomer Elohim le-Noach ket kol-basar

ARTHUR. Okay. Okay. Now it needs to rise here. Gosh, I'm starving. Are you hungry?

NELSON. I could use a little cereal.

ARTHUR. Bring it out! We'll eat while we work.

NELSON. *(scrambling to get boxes of cereal)* I'll bring them all. And we can have a little of each.

ARTHUR. We have a lot of work to do, Nelson. I think we're going to have to work every day after school to get you ready. I want you to sing those other boys under the Bema.

NELSON. That's great sir. I'll be here. Every day.

(Light shift.)

(RACHEL *and* **STEPHEN HAWKING** *are sitting behind Starbucks.* **RACHEL** *is stoned, smoking her funny cigarette and drinking a mochachino.)*

STEPHEN. You kissed him?

RACHEL. Seven times. What does it mean?

STEPHEN. It's not really my area of expertise.

RACHEL. Yeah. Me either.

(Pause while they chew this over.)

I loved your book. So much. So much, Stephen. Can I call you Stephen?

STEPHEN. Call me Dr. Hawking.

RACHEL. You make sense of…everything. Of the universe. It all always seemed so incomprehensible and pointless to me. Where *did* we come from? Why are we here? I don't know. But it makes me feel that someday we might know.

STEPHEN. The cake is in the search. Finding out is the icing.

RACHEL. Wow. Did you write that?

STEPHEN. No. It's your funny cigarettes.

RACHEL. Nelson says it's a wonderful time to be alive. Isn't that amazing? That he really feels that way? I always thought that optimism and joy were a sign of low intellect. But he seems fairly bright. When I'm with him, I almost feel hopeful. But then I go home and my mother is waiting for the apocalypse like it's a Greyhound Bus.

STEPHEN. Well, we do need to work on an alternative.

RACHEL. To what?

STEPHEN. Earth.

RACHEL. Earth?

STEPHEN. The end *is* coming.

RACHEL. Oh my God! Even my hallucinations are raving. I am so fucked up!

STEPHEN. It's all about you, isn't it? Didn't you read any of the transcripts from my Symposium?

RACHEL. What did they say?

STEPHEN. We have maybe one hundred years.

RACHEL. And then what? The Rapture?

STEPHEN. An enormous rogue meteorite. A genetically engineered virus. Sudden global warming. Nuclear War.

RACHEL. But not the Rapture, right?

STEPHEN. The human race needs to spread out into space for the survival of the species. We can have a permanent base on the moon in 20 years. If we get cracking.

RACHEL. But Stephen, why not just let it all go? Human annihilation. Maybe something more intelligent will grow – less destructive.

STEPHEN. Survival of the species is one of our most basic human instincts. You should really think about why you kissed Nelson. And read my papers – buy them and read them. And give your mother a break. We're all looking for answers.

(He starts backing out.)

RACHEL. Don't leave. I have so much to ask you.

STEPHEN. You're bringing me down, man.

(He rolls away.)

(Light shift. The church bell chimes three times. The Stein living room, late at night. There is a thunder and lightning storm. The sound of rain. Offstage we hear **SYLVIA** *calling out softly.)*

SYLVIA. Jesus, where are you?

(A hall light comes on. **SYLVIA** *comes out to the kitchen in her nightgown.)*

Jesus? Are you there?

(He comes out of the shadows.)

Oh Jesus! Thank God. I was so scared. I just woke up and I didn't know where you were. I thought it was happening. I thought I'd been left behind.

(She goes to him and he takes her in his arms.)

JESUS. Did you have a bad dream?

SYLVIA. There was a storm, like tonight. Thunder and explosions. The sky was on fire. I heard screaming and I was trying to find Rachel and Arthur, but I couldn't. So I prayed that you would come and take me in your arms. And you did.

(realizing)

Just like now. You took me in your arms and you whispered, "It's time, Sylvia."

JESUS. *(whispering)* It's time Sylvia.

SYLVIA. Tonight? Now?

JESUS. Soon.

SYLVIA. This is so much like my dream. Is this my dream?

JESUS. Soon.

SYLVIA. When, Jesus? Please. I need to know.

JESUS. But of that day and that hour knoweth no man, no, not the angels which are in heaven…

JESUS & SYLVIA. Neither the Son, but the Father.

JESUS. Just keep preparing.

SYLVIA. All right.

(a moment)

But, you must have some idea when it will be.

JESUS. Sylvia.

SYLVIA. Could you just give me a general idea?

JESUS. Soon.

SYLVIA. A little less general? I know. I shall not knoweth. I know. But I feel this panic, Jesus. That it will all start happening. That I won't know where Rachel is. That she'll be off at school, or at the library, or wherever it is she goes now, I don't even know. And it will all start happening, and I won't be able to get to her. To take her with me. Or…Or…to say goodbye. Please Jesus. Just…Just blink. Okay?

JESUS. Blink?

SYLVIA. Once if I guess wrong, and twice if I guess right.

JESUS. Sylvia. This is not a game.

SYLVIA. Please. Just a blink. What could a blink hurt?

JESUS. You need more faith, Sylvia.

SYLVIA. I know, but I'm so anxious. I don't think I'll sleep again unless I know something for sure. Now, I'm just going to say some days. One for "No," two for "Yes."

JESUS. This isn't right.

SYLVIA. Is it going to happen tonight?

(There is a long pause. And then **JESUS** *blinks once.)*

Was that a blink? Jesus, was it?

*(***JESUS*** remains stony faced.)*

It was! It was a single blink! It's not tonight. Thank you Jesus. Thank you so much! Okay. Tomorrow. Monday.

*(***JESUS*** blinks once.)*

SYLVIA. One blink. Tuesday?

*(***JESUS*** blinks once.)*

Was that one blink or two? For Tuesday? I'm sorry, I couldn't tell.

*(***JESUS*** again blinks once.)*

Not Tuesday! Wednesday?

*(***JESUS*** pauses, then blinks twice – or was it something in his eye?)*

(stunned)

Jesus. You just blinked twice, didn't you– you blinked twice for Wednesday. Or was that something in your eye? Could you do it again?

JESUS. I don't like this, Sylvia.

SYLVIA. All right. It's Wednesday. The apocalypse is coming Wednesday. End days. The Rapture. Armageddon. My dream was right. Wasn't it?

JESUS. Just keep doing your good works. Spread the good

news. Save as many people as you possibly can.

SYLVIA. What about Rachel, Jesus? Will she be coming too?

JESUS. I can't say.

SYLVIA. Oh, please. She asked for your forgiveness. You heard her today in church.

JESUS. It was under some duress.

SYLVIA. But she did say it. Shouldn't that count?

JESUS. I don't think she really meant it, Sylvia. Not in her heart.

SYLVIA. Oh, Jesus. She's a teenager. You know how they are. Please forgive Rachel and Arthur. Please don't leave them behind.

JESUS. We'll see. Goodbye, Sylvia.

SYLVIA. Goodbye? Where are you going? Don't go.

JESUS. I have to go to come back. Right?

SYLVIA. Can't you go Tuesday and come back Wednesday?

JESUS. You don't need me with you every minute now, Sylvia. You're past that. You can carry me in your heart, now. You can do the good works in my name.

SYLVIA. You're mad at me, aren't you, Jesus? I shouldn't have pushed you so hard. I always do that. I'm very pushy.

JESUS. You're a good person, Sylvia.

SYLVIA. I am?

JESUS. You're a good person, and you're doing good in the world.

SYLVIA. Thank you, Jesus.

JESUS. All right then.

SYLVIA. Can you just come back at night and help me get to sleep? Can you sit with me while I pray?

JESUS. You pray, and I'll listen. You dream, and I'll be in your dreams. I'll come back for you when I come back for all the saved.

SYLVIA. I'm scared.

JESUS. Have faith, Sylvia.

SYLVIA. I love you, Jesus.

JESUS. I love you too.

(**JESUS** *leaves.*)

SYLVIA. Come back for me.

(**SYLVIA** *stands alone as the lights fade till we see only the ghostly glow of her nightgown.*)

(*Lights down.*)

End of Act I

ACT II

(The Church Bell chimes four times. Lights up. Monday afternoon. **SYLVIA**, **ARTHUR** *and* **RACHEL** *are all in the kitchen.)*

RACHEL. So…now you're a prophet.

SYLVIA. It's not important how I know. I just know.

RACHEL. Have you told anyone else about this?

SYLVIA. Just a few people.

RACHEL. Who?

SYLVIA. I told Reverend Peter and the congregation.

RACHEL. Okay.

SYLVIA. And I put an ad in the Penny Saver.

RACHEL. Was your name on it?

SYLVIA. Of course not.

RACHEL. Okay.

SYLVIA. And I handed out flyers in front of Shoprite today.

RACHEL. Oh my God, Mom! What did they say?

SYLVIA. The Rapture is coming this Wednesday. Repent and be saved.

RACHEL. Oh, my God. I'll never be able to leave the house again.

SYLVIA. I'm trying to save as many people as I can. I'm trying to do good in the world. Will you wait with me Wednesday?

RACHEL. I have a Social Studies quiz Wednesday.

SYLVIA. It's not going to matter, Honey. None of this is going to matter.

RACHEL. But when you're wrong, I'll have to make it up Thursday during study hall, which means I won't be able to audit physics, which I'm going to do now, by the way.

SYLVIA. There won't be any Thursday. The Rapture will

have started, and there will be chaos on Earth and we'll be gone.

ARTHUR. I just bought milk. Will it keep while we're gone?

SYLVIA. We won't need milk where we're going.

RACHEL. You bought milk?

ARTHUR. I went grocery shopping today.

(RACHEL goes to the refrigerator and opens the door.)

RACHEL. Oh my God It's full! There's lunch meat. Cheese! Apples! Oranges! Yogurt! Wow. Thanks Dad!

(She goes to him and gives him a hug. For the first time in a long time. He's very moved.)

ARTHUR. You make a list, Rach. Every day you make a list. And I'll go back and get whatever you want.

(to **SYLVIA***)* You too, Honey.

SYLVIA. We'll be gone Wednesday. We won't want for anything.

RACHEL. Is there bread?

ARTHUR. Check the bread box.

(She does. Jumping up and down like a little kid.)

RACHEL. Rye! Yay! I'm going to make a ham and cheese sandwich! There's mustard. Yay!! Does anyone else want a sandwich?

ARTHUR. I could use a half.

RACHEL. I'll split one with you. Baloney! Wow! This is so excellent. Mom, you want one?

SYLVIA. No, Hon. Will you stay with me?

RACHEL. Won't Jesus be able to find me at school?

SYLVIA. I need to have you with me. I need to know that we're all going. Together. That we're all going.

(There's a knock on the door.)

NELSON. Mr. S.?

(NELSON enters.)

Hey! Everybody!

RACHEL. There's food! You want a sandwich?

NELSON. Food?

RACHEL. My Dad went shopping.

NELSON. Mr. S.! By yourself?

ARTHUR. I made three trips.

NELSON. That is so awesome!

RACHEL. You want a sandwich?

NELSON. Sure. Can I help?

RACHEL. Spread the mustard.

SYLVIA. Will you stay with me, Arthur?

ARTHUR. Yes, Sylvia.

RACHEL. Pickles! For the list.

ARTHUR. Got it!

SYLVIA. Rachel? Will you stay?

NELSON. Where are we staying?

RACHEL. You didn't get the memo?

NELSON. What?

RACHEL. Jesus told my mom…

SYLVIA. Nobody *told* me, Honey. He didn't *tell* me.

RACHEL. The Rapture is coming Wednesday.

NELSON. We have a history of U.S. Government quiz Wednesday.

SYLVIA. There's not going to be any history. There's not going to be any U.S. There's not going to be any government. I know this is hard for all of you to accept, but all our earthly needs will vanish.

NELSON. What's going to happen exactly?

SYLVIA. Well, first the dead forgiven will rise.

RACHEL. From their graves?

NELSON. What was that movie? Where the dead people rise up from their graves?

SYLVIA. Their *souls*.

RACHEL. "Night of the Living Dead." Ughhh.

SYLVIA. Their *souls* will rise. And then Jesus will come with a shout, with the voice of the archangel and the trumpet of God, and the living will rise to the clouds to meet the Lord in the air.

NELSON. Cool. Count me in Mrs. S.

RACHEL. We have school.

NELSON. But we have school every day. This seems like a once in a lifetime event. What time does it all start?

SYLVIA. We'll begin our vigil at midnight on Tuesday.

NELSON. Should I bring anything?

RACHEL. That's it? You're in? She says the world is ending and you start packing your bags?

NELSON. Do we need to pack?

RACHEL. What are you going to tell your stepparents? Won't they think it's weird if you leave the house at midnight?

NELSON. They're still kind of in that honeymoon phase. So…they don't keep all that good track. Should I bring something? I make a really nice dip with onion soup mix and water chestnuts.

ARTHUR. I'll pick up some chips. Maybe a veggie platter.

SYLVIA. We're going to be praying. And repenting.

NELSON. Definitely.

ARTHUR. And I'll make everybody waffles for breakfast.

SYLVIA. We're going to be reading the Bible.

ARTHUR. Nelson, I'll finally get to teach you gin. Or, wait! There are four of us! We could play Hearts.

SYLVIA. No cards, Arthur. What is wrong with you today?

ARTHUR. *(over this)* Your mother used to be a killer Hearts player. Remember, Hon.? Our third year at N.Y.U.? We called her the shark.

RACHEL. Really?

ARTHUR. We used to wager copying fees at the student center, and your mother and I…

SYLVIA. We're not going to have time to play games, Arthur.

ARTHUR. But it's the whole day, right? We'll all be here a long time together.

NELSON. Unless Jesus comes like, right after Midnight.

ARTHUR. It'll be great. Nelson, bring your guitar.

SYLVIA. This isn't a party! This is your last chance to repent. To be saved. And when he comes, you won't need to play games. You'll be free. You'll feel joyful and loved.

ARTHUR. I do feel loved.

(He goes to put his arm around her. She shrinks away from him, involuntarily, repulsed.)

(There is a quiet moment when everyone takes this in.)

SYLVIA. Rachel? Will you stay?

RACHEL. Why?

SYLVIA. Haven't I explained this??

RACHEL. No. Why do you want me? Why do you want Dad? It doesn't seem like you can stand the sight of us here. Why do you want us there?

SYLVIA. Of course I want you here.

RACHEL. You want our souls. The rest of us you could do without.

SYLVIA. That's not true.

RACHEL. What happens when Jesus doesn't come?

SYLVIA. He's going to come.

RACHEL. But what if he doesn't?

SYLVIA. I have complete faith in him.

NELSON. Stay, Rachel.

RACHEL. You think Jesus is going to come for us?

NELSON. I don't know. But we already know what happens if we go to school. Now we'll find out what happens if we don't.

RACHEL. We'll be marked absent. That's what happens.

ARTHUR. I'll make Reuben sandwiches for lunch.

RACHEL. This is wrong, Dad. You know it's all crazy.

ARTHUR. We'll all be together. All four of us. For twenty-four hours. We'll be a family.

RACHEL. And then what?

NELSON. Stay, Rachel.

RACHEL. Mom. If he doesn't come – will you give it all up?

ARTHUR. Rachel. Don't do that to your mother.

RACHEL. But if she's so sure…once there's proof that she's wrong…

NELSON. Rabbi Baumbach says faith doesn't need proof. If there's proof it isn't faith.

ARTHUR. That's very smart. He sounds very smart.

RACHEL. What are you talking about? You're an atheist.

ARTHUR. I was observant at one point in my life.

RACHEL. You were? What happened?

ARTHUR. I got busy. Working. Making money. Starting a family.

RACHEL. You gave it up for her.

ARTHUR. No.

RACHEL. You did. She wanted you to stop, and you caved.

ARTHUR. Other things became important. I made choices.

RACHEL. It always has to be her way.

SYLVIA. Rachel. If you'll stay Wednesday, if you'll really repent…

RACHEL. Yeah?

SYLVIA. In your heart…

RACHEL. Yeah?

SYLVIA. If Jesus doesn't come by midnight, I'll stop. All of it.

ARTHUR. You don't have to do that Sylvia.

SYLVIA. I know he'll come. Please wait with me, Rachel. Having you off at school when it all happens – I just won't be able to stand it. It'll be that day all over again. All the chaos and panic and I won't know if you're all right. Please.

(pause)

RACHEL. *(a breath)* Swiss Cheese? On the Reuben?

ARTHUR. Of course. And pastrami. And sour kraut.

RACHEL. I'll stay.

(Light down.)

(Tuesday night. Lights up on SYLVIA, RACHEL and ARTHUR sitting at the kitchen table. They each have a Bible opened in front of them.)

RACHEL. *(whispering to* **ARTHUR***)* What about now?

ARTHUR. *(whispering back.)* Eighteen after.

RACHEL. That's it??

SYLVIA. Read.

RACHEL. I am. I'm reading.

ARTHUR. Maybe we should eat a little something. Anybody else hungry?

SYLVIA. Shhhh.

> *(looking over at his Bible)*

Arthur. You're not even on the right book. Go to Revelations.

> *(She sighs deeply and goes back to her bible.)*

ARTHUR. Oh! Sorry.

> *(***ARTHUR*** searches for the right page. Reaches into his pocket and pulls out his glasses.)*

Guess what? I found my glasses yesterday.

RACHEL. Yeah?

SYLVIA. Good. Put them on. Read.

RACHEL. Where were they?

ARTHUR. In my briefcase.

RACHEL. You hadn't looked in there? All this time?

ARTHUR. It was files of paperwork from people…they don't exist any more. All those names.

RACHEL. God, Dad.

ARTHUR. It was strange. It seemed completely unconnected to me. Like I was looking through someone else's things. It's hard to believe that was my life.

RACHEL. You were brave.

ARTHUR. Nah.

RACHEL. To look in there. Yes, you were.

ARTHUR. Well, I'm glad to have my glasses back. Though I think my prescription's changed.

SYLVIA. Try. Please. Just try to read.

RACHEL. Okay.

ARTHUR. Sorry.

(They try for a moment.)

RACHEL. *(whispering)* What about now?

ARTHUR. *(whispering)* Almost twenty-two after.

RACHEL. *(whispering)* That's it???

(**NELSON** *bursts in. He is no longer dressed as Elvis. His hair is not slicked back. He is wearing jeans and a T-shirt, carrying a paper bag, a tupperware container of dip and his guitar. He is a bundle of anxious, neurotic energy. He speaks breathlessly, with little pause.*)

NELSON. Hi! Everybody. Rachel. Hi. Sorry I'm late. I've got some really bad news.

(He bends over to catch his breath while everyone stares at him.)

No water chestnuts. I mix the sour cream with the soup mix, go to the cabinet – nothing. Not even a four ounce can! So, I run to the Shoprite which should never be closed since the sign says 24/7, and it was closed! Can you believe that? I mean, *can we count on the Shoprite or not?!* I considered going door to door asking for water chestnuts, but I worried that at this hour it might not be appropriate, so I went back home, got the dip as it is and brought it anyway but it's just not going to be as good as if I'd made it with the water chestnuts so... sorry.

RACHEL. Where's your costume?

NELSON. It's here. In this paper bag.

RACHEL. Why?

NELSON. In case I get a little nervous. I used to get a little nervous, or *jumpy* really, loquacious, if I wasn't wearing it, but I don't think I'm going to need to wear it any more.

RACHEL. Why not?

NELSON. You said I shouldn't.

RACHEL. I don't want you to not wear it for me.

NELSON. So should I wear it?

RACHEL. You have to decide for yourself.

NELSON. Well, I did. I mean, I decided for myself to do it for you.

RACHEL. I don't want you to do it for me.

NELSON. Okay. Well, I think I am doing it for myself.

RACHEL. Okay.

NELSON. And my new step-father, Ben, he's kind of having a hard time with the outfit.

(Breathless. He rocks back and forth and paces as he speaks.)

And Rabbi Baumbach was thinking the outfit might not be so great at the actual Bar Mitzvah. I mean, he doesn't have a problem with me wearing it to Hebrew School or anything, though the parents of the other kids expressed some concern that it's distracting.

ARTHUR. You seem a little jumpy.

NELSON. No, no. I'm fine. But mostly, ever since you said that I should stop wearing it it's got me to thinking, I mean, I'd leap into a burning building for you no question *so why wouldn't I just stop wearing the outfit?! What's important to me?! Make a choice!* Although, in some ways, the burning building might be a little easier. Quicker, for example?

RACHEL. *(caught up in his panic)* Put on the fucking outfit, for Christ's sakes!

SYLVIA. Rachel!

RACHEL. Sorry. Put on the outfit.

NELSON. Do you want me to?

RACHEL. ACHHHH!!!

ARTHUR. Maybe put on the belt. Would that help? If you put on the belt?

NELSON. It might.

RACHEL. Put on the friggin' belt!

SYLVIA. Rachel!

RACHEL. Sorry.

*(**NELSON** scrambles through the bag and retrieves the glittery Elvis belt. He tries to put it through his jeans*

loops, but it's too wide. His hands are shaking the shake of the addict off his fix as he struggles.)

NELSON. Gosh! I think you might be right, Mr. S! I think I might be just a little jumpy.

RACHEL. Oh, for Pete's sakes!

(She grabs the belt from him and buckles it around his waist.)

There.

NELSON. *(Breathes a deep sigh. A wave of relief floods his entire body until he is limp.)* Thanks. That's good. That's better. Thanks.

(RACHEL studies him for a moment. Ruffles his hair a bit. Steps back to regard him.)

RACHEL. You look good. Like this. I like it.

NELSON. Yeah?

RACHEL. It's good.

NELSON. Thanks.

(There is a brief hush. The phone rings.)

ARTHUR. At this hour we're getting a call?

(SYLVIA answers it.)

SYLVIA. Hello?

ARTHUR. Is somebody dead?

SYLVIA. No, Mrs. Henson. Nothing's happened. Not yet.

RACHEL. Rapture hotline.

SYLVIA. I'll let you know. As soon as I do. Okay. God bless you, Mrs. Henson.

(She hangs up.)

ARTHUR. Should we crack open that dip?

SYLVIA. We should pray.

ARTHUR. And then we can have the dip after?

SYLVIA. Maybe.

ARTHUR. I bought some of those exotic chips – you know, they're made of yams and beets and unexpected things like that.

SYLVIA. All right. Everyone gather around.

RACHEL. Did you get any plain chips?

ARTHUR. Oh yeah. I got a variety.

SYLVIA. Stop talking about chips! I mean honestly. Let's pray!

RACHEL. Okay. Let's pray.

NELSON. Definitely. I printed out some stuff from Rapture-Alert.com. Very cool website. Have you visited it Mrs. S.?

SYLVIA. No. Thank you Nelson. Maybe we can look at that later.

(She looks through her knapsack and pulls out several sheets of prayers.)

Here are some things Reverend Peter pieced together for me from Corinthians and Mark.

ARTHUR. And then maybe Nelson could do some of his Torah portion. It's fantastic. He sounds just like an old Jew.

NELSON. Mr. S.

ARTHUR. The dovening. The intonation. It's like I'm listening to my Uncle Morty.

SYLVIA. "Lord Jesus, I invite you into my heart anew today, and I ask forgiveness for all of my sins. Jesus, thank you for dying for my sins and for forgiving me of them through your shed blood on the cross. Please take away all the sinful "old things" in my heart that defile me, especially – Fill in the Blank.

RACHEL. Fill in the blank?

SYLVIA. You know how you've sinned, Rachel. Ask for forgiveness.

NELSON. This is tough.

SYLVIA. Think about your regrets.

NELSON. I feel really bad about the water chestnuts.

ARTHUR. I bet this boy doesn't have a thing in his life to regret.

SYLVIA. *Just ask forgiveness all right!?* Could you all just ask Jesus for forgiveness? This really doesn't have to be so complicated! If you could all just FOCUS and get your minds off dip and waffles and chips and your Uncle Morty, if you could all just FOCUS, maybe you could be forgiven and saved and raptured and not left to burn in the fiery furnace of hell on Earth!!! Okay?

NELSON. Got it!

SYLVIA. "Please take away all the sinful "old things" in my heart that defile me, especially ____

(She looks around ominously. They are all silent.)

And send your Holy Spirit afresh into my life to help me, heal me, lead me and transform me. In Jesus Christ I pray, Amen."

(They all wait for a moment, afraid to be wrong, then answer with "Amen.")

ARTHUR. So, good! So we prayed! Let's have a nosh!

SYLVIA. Let's see if anything's started happening yet.

(She turns on the TV, turns the sound down and sits raptly watching the silent picture.)

NELSON. That static? They think some of it is electronic noise produced by the Big Bang over 13.7 billion years ago.

RACHEL. My parents just won't pay for cable.

(During the following **ARTHUR,** **NELSON** *and* **RACHEL** *pour bags of chips into bowls, get the dip ready, etc.)*

NELSON. You think it'll be on the news, Mrs. S.?

RACHEL. Well if graves start getting uncovered and bodies start floating out...

ARTHUR. There will be that trumpet playing, right? That should be a dead give-away, if we hear the trumpet playing.

NELSON. You know, I've got some stuff printed out from the website. Sort of a checklist.

RACHEL. These yam chips are actually very good.

ARTHUR. The dip is excellent. You know what we need?

RACHEL. Carrots.

ARTHUR. A nice piece of salami.

NELSON. Here it is. "Immediately after the tribulation of those days shall the sun be darkened, the moon shall not give her light, and the stars shall fall from heaven, and the powers of the heavens shall be shaken."

ARTHUR. Nelson, give a look. Is the moon shining?

(He does.)

NELSON. So far.

ARTHUR. So we're good. The moon is shining and no trumpets. Let's play cards!

SYLVIA. *(sending him a look that could kill)* How would everybody feel about a movie?

RACHEL. Are you kidding? I would love a movie!

NELSON. Excellent Mrs. S.

SYLVIA. Reverend Peter loaned me a couple of videos.

RACHEL. Oh.

*(**SYLVIA** pulls one out of her knapsack.)*

Oh. Kirk Cameron.

SYLVIA. You know him?

RACHEL. He was on that sitcom.

SYLVIA. Then we'll start with this.

*(**SYLVIA** puts in "Left Behind" as everyone gathers. **RACHEL** and **ARTHUR** sit on the tiny couch. **NELSON** and **SYLVIA** take the chairs.)*

RACHEL. They show those awful reruns. What was it?

NELSON. "Growing Pains."

*(The phone rings. **SYLVIA** answers it. The following overlaps.)*

SYLVIA. Hello? Oh, hi, Mr. Elmower. No, not yet. We're about to watch "Left Behind."

NELSON. You didn't like that show?

RACHEL. Ughh.

SYLVIA. Reverend Peter says it's wonderful too. All right. I'll let you know as soon as I do. God Bless you too.

NELSON. I liked all of them. Partridge Family, Brady Bunch, Family Ties, Leave it to Beaver, Father Knows Best.

RACHEL. Geek.

SYLVIA. Shhh. It's coming on.

(They watch for a few moments as the movie starts. We hear opening-credit music.)

This will give you a better idea of what might happen. If you're left behind.

RACHEL. *(yawning)* I'm getting sleepy.

*(She rests her head on **ARTHUR**. He puts his arm around her, and she snuggles in, falling asleep.)*

NELSON. We should read the books. They're supposed to be real page-turners.

SYLVIA. Well, if we had more time. Here it is.

*(**ARTHUR**'s head has fallen back and he is nearly asleep too.)*

SYLVIA. Rachel. It's starting. Arthur. Come on now. Wake up.

ARTHUR. *(asleep)* I'm awake.

NELSON. *(to **SYLVIA**)* The hour, not the company, right?

SYLVIA. I really wanted them to see this.

NELSON. We'll fill them in. I'll pay close attention.

(He leans back to watch. Though he fights it, his eyes want to close.)

Oh boy. Sorry. Just smack me. Okay? If I start to doze.

*(But little by little he gives in to sleep. **SYLVIA** remains rapt on the screen. Taut. On alert. Lights fade.)*

*(Lights back up. Hours later. There is the fuzzy static of the TV. **SYLVIA** sits staring off. The other three are asleep.)*

NELSON. *(murmuring in his sleep)* Mom…Mommy.

(A shout which wakens him.)

Mom!

(Looking around, startled and disoriented. Realizing.)

Oh. Hey. Mrs. S. I must have dozed off. Did I miss anything?

(**SYLVIA** *shakes her head, no.*)

Wow. Four-thirty-six. Sorry. How was the movie?

(**SYLVIA** *just nods.*)

Really wish I'd seen it. Maybe I can borrow it some time. Or…oh. Right. Well, maybe we could watch it again later.

(**SYLVIA** *just stares off.*)

Are you okay, Mrs. S.?

The waiting is hard. I know. I hate waiting.

Do you want to take a little nap? I'll stay up. I'll wake you the second something happens. You want to be nice and rested when he comes, right?

Mrs. S.?

SYLVIA. Nelson. Do you think Rachel really repented in church Sunday?

NELSON. Well, she asked for forgiveness. You heard her.

SYLVIA. But did she mean it in her heart?

NELSON. I kind of think she said it so you'd let her go back to school.

SYLVIA. Do you think she'll be saved?

NELSON. Jesus has to know for someone like Rachel, just saying it counts for more.

SYLVIA. I think she's going to be left behind, Nelson. I don't think she and Arthur will be saved.

NELSON. Really?

SYLVIA. Don't tell her that.

NELSON. No. Of course not.

SYLVIA. I'm so afraid. If they're left behind, I don't know. I don't know what I'll do.

NELSON. That's tough. I know for sure I'm not going if Rachel's not going.

SYLVIA. You know that?

NELSON. It just wouldn't be Heaven for me without her.

SYLVIA. You've only known Rachel a couple of weeks. Right?

NELSON. Yeah. How long have you known Jesus?

SYLVIA. Three months. And seventeen days.

NELSON. I guess sometimes you just know, huh?

SYLVIA. He's completely changed my life. If you'd known me before, Nelson. I was such a different person.

NELSON. Yeah?

SYLVIA. I questioned everything. I was really angry and competitive and judgmental and controlling. I never want to be like that again.

NELSON. Yeah.

SYLVIA. And then after what happened – you know?

NELSON. Yeah.

SYLVIA. That whole day I thought Arthur was dead. I couldn't find him. All the people he worked with gone. People I'd just seen a week before. Gone. I thought he was gone too.

NELSON. Yeah.

SYLVIA. I just don't trust the world any more, Nelson. I don't want to be here any more.

NELSON. You mean…Earth?

SYLVIA. I want to be somewhere safe.

NELSON. I don't know. I really like it here.

SYLVIA. You're not afraid of death?

NELSON. Rabbi Baumbach says that knowing death is inevitable gives every moment of life meaning.

SYLVIA. He said that?

NELSON. Well, I don't think he was the first to say it. But I like it. Life isn't too bad. And even the bad stuff is interesting.

SYLVIA. But if you weren't saved, you'd be eternally damned on Earth. Satan will take away all your joy anyway.

NELSON. I think if I'm with Rachel, I'll still be happy. And with Mr. S. And you too. It seems like an awful sacrifice to lose any of you. And Rabbi Baumbach. He's, you know, he's a really good guy. I could never imagine that guy doing anything mean to anybody. So, it really seems wrong that he wouldn't get to go.

SYLVIA. Maybe he'll repent. At the final hour. Maybe they'll all repent when they see it's true.

NELSON. But if they didn't, I'd have to tell Jesus that I was sorry, but I wasn't sorry. That I needed to stay here. Wouldn't you?

SYLVIA. I love him so much.

NELSON. I hope it doesn't come to that. I hope you don't have to make that choice.

(Lights shift. Morning. SYLVIA *is still staring off.* RACHEL *and* NELSON *are asleep.)*

ARTHUR. Morning hon. My arm – Ow ow ow.

(He tries to move it without waking RACHEL*.)*

Guess we kind of petered out on you last night, huh.

Whoa. It's almost lunchtime. You feel like waffles?

*(*ARTHUR *extricates himself from the sleeping* RACHEL *and sees that there is white makeup on his shirt where* RACHEL *lay.)*

It's nice to know that white stuff comes off.

(Shaking his arm out.)

Oh, hey. Did anything happen last night?

SYLVIA. Are you mocking me?

ARTHUR. I'm sorry. I don't mean to do that.

SYLVIA. But you don't believe in any of it, do you?

ARTHUR. I believe in you.

(She's silent.)

So, if I make them will you eat some? Or should I wait for the kids?

SYLVIA. What?

ARTHUR. Waffles.

SYLVIA. I'm not hungry.

ARTHUR. *(studies her for a moment)* It's going to be okay.

SYLVIA. What is?

ARTHUR. Us. Rachel. I know I've really let you down. For a long time. But I'm going to make it up to you. If you let me. If it's not too late.

(SYLVIA is silent.)

I'll go make the waffles. And if you get hungry, you can have some.

(Lights shift – hours later. Everyone is sitting around the living room, snacking. SYLVIA is sitting with her Bible in her lap, reading.)

NELSON. Well, because light takes so long to travel, when we're observing something billions of miles away, we really are seeing events that happened billions of years ago. So actually we *are* looking into the distant past.

ARTHUR. This is unbelievable. Do you hear this, Hon? We can see to billions of years ago.

RACHEL. Mom doesn't believe there was a billions of years ago any more. She thinks God created it all six thousand years ago, and before that, bupkis. All that dinosaur carbon sampling is a lot of crazy voodoo.

ARTHUR. Yeah?

SYLVIA. You know what I think, Arthur. Don't play stupid.

ARTHUR. I'm not playing.

RACHEL. Tell him about LISA.

ARTHUR. Who's Lisa?

NELSON. The Laser Interferometer Space Antenna.

ARTHUR. The who?

RACHEL. This is amazing. I don't even understand it really, but it blows my mind.

NELSON. It's these three hockey-puck shaped spacecraft connected by laser beams, that will be released about three million miles apart. And they'll search for gravitational waves.

ARTHUR. And why would they do that? It sounds very expensive.

NELSON. It'll answer a lot of mind-blowing questions, Mr. S. Like, how did the universe begin? Does space have edges? Does time have a beginning and an end?

ARTHUR. I never even knew I had those questions, right, Honey?

RACHEL. Well, soon, you'll have answers.

NELSON. They're hoping to launch it in 2015.

RACHEL. Soon, every question we've ever asked will have observable answers. Empirical proof. And then we'll have a whole new slew of questions. I mean, it's limitless – how much we could learn. Why would you believe in God, when believing in science is thoroughly awe-inspiring.

SYLVIA. You do everything you can think of to hurt me, Rachel – but, it's not about me. It's about *your* relationship to Jesus. It's about *your* salvation. It's about *your* soul.

RACHEL. Mom, can't you give up on my soul? It would be such a relief if you could just believe what you believe – I'll try not to be such a total ass about it, if you could just give up on my soul. Just let me not get saved.

SYLVIA. I can't do that, Rachel.

RACHEL. Why?

SYLVIA. That's like asking me to watch you run in front of a speeding bus, and not rush out to save you. I'm your mother. I love you. I need to save you.

(There is a flash of lightning and, close after, a crack of thunder. The lights go out.)

RACHEL. *(in the dark)* Holy shit! What was that?

NELSON. Was that the trumpet?

ARTHUR. I think we're having a little electrical storm.

SYLVIA. No. This is it. It's happening.

(The lights flicker. Another flash and thunder clap.)

RACHEL. Jesus! That's close.

SYLVIA. Rachel, watch your mouth!

NELSON. You think this is the beginning of the end, Mrs. S.?

SYLVIA. I know it. It's starting.

(The lights flicker back on. The phone rings. **SYLVIA** *answers it.)*

Hello? Carla?

RACHEL. Yikes. See if the TV is working.

SYLVIA. *(on the phone)* I think so too. All right, Carla. God bless. See you soon.

ARTHUR. They say it's a tornado.

SYLVIA. They don't know.

RACHEL. Wow. Was this in the forecast?

NELSON. I don't think so.

SYLVIA. This is it. I can feel it. It's starting.

ARTHUR. Where are the flashlights? In case the power goes out again.

RACHEL. Second drawer. I'll get some candles.

(another flash and crack)

(The following overlaps.)

SYLVIA. Rachel. Do you accept Jesus as your personal lord and savior?

RACHEL. Come on, Mom. We've been through this and through this.

ARTHUR. *(the flashlights)* They're not here.

SYLVIA. *(growing urgency)* Just say it. Please.

RACHEL. I said it. Try the first drawer, Dad. I know they're in one of them.

SYLVIA. Say it again.

RACHEL. Mom, it's pointless. You know who I am.

ARTHUR. Huh. Not here either.

SYLVIA. *(in a panic)* You agreed to stay here with me. To wait for him.

RACHEL. Well, I've got the candles. Just get some matches.

ARTHUR. And they would be…

RACHEL. Next to the stove.

SYLVIA. It's all meaningless if you don't repent.

RACHEL. I'm not going to say it again.

SYLVIA. *(getting more and more frantic)* Rachel. I don't want to go without you. Tell Jesus that you really mean it in your heart.

RACHEL. Mom.

ARTHUR. Gottem.

SYLVIA. *(sobbing)* It's not too late. Please, Rachel.

RACHEL. Oh God, Mom.

SYLVIA. Honey, I can't lose you. Please.

RACHEL. Okay, okay! I mean it in my heart!

SYLVIA. Thank you. Thank you Rachel. Pray, everyone. This is it. Let's all pray.

*(**SYLVIA** falls to her knees and begins praying. **NELSON** joins her on the floor.)*

ARTHUR. *(still watching the TV)* Power's out down county. But they say it should move through fast.

(Another flash of lightning and clap of thunder. The sound of pelting hail.)

RACHEL. Oh my God, is that hail? In September?

NELSON. Sounds like stars falling, right?

SYLVIA. Rachel join us. Come pray.

(lightning and thunder)

RACHEL. Come on Dad.

*(She gets down beside **NELSON** and **SYLVIA.** The phone starts ringing, then the lights go out and the phone stops.)*

SYLVIA. Jesus. We're ready for you.

*(**ARTHUR** is trying to light the match.)*

ARTHUR. Ow!

SYLVIA. Please come for us, Jesus. We all repent our wicked, sinful ways.

*(**ARTHUR** lights a candle. Everyone is lit by the glow.)*

We're all grateful for the sacrifices you made for us, Jesus. We're ready to be saved. We're ready to join you.

(The lights come back up. The hail is replaced by a gentle rain. The TV is back on.)

(ARTHUR *blows out the candle.)*

ARTHUR. Looks like it's blown over. They say it's moving North.

RACHEL. *(very unnerved and bewildered)* Wasn't that wild? Hail in September?

NELSON. Yeah.

RACHEL. That sudden storm like that? It was so close. Wasn't that weird?

ARTHUR. Global warming. It's serious. I mean, have we ever had a summer like this past one?

NELSON. The polar ice caps are melting.

RACHEL. But, I mean, had they predicted that storm? In the forecast?

NELSON. I don't think so.

RACHEL. That hail was like golf balls. I was afraid it was going to crack a window.

ARTHUR. Very scary.

RACHEL. It was weird.

(There is a pause.)

ARTHUR. Anybody up for a Reuben sandwich?

(SYLVIA *looks at him with hatred.)*

RACHEL. Excellent.

NELSON. Sounds great, Mr. S.

(They go to join him in the kitchen. **SYLVIA** *remains on her knees, seething.)*

RACHEL. You got the Swiss cheese?

ARTHUR. I got everything. And brownies for dessert.

RACHEL. No way.

(realizing **SYLVIA** *is not with them)*

Mom? You want a Reuben?

(SYLVIA *does not answer. She remains kneeling, furious.)*

NELSON. Mrs. S.?

ARTHUR. *(to* **RACHEL** *and* **NELSON***)* Get out the bread and the fixings, and I'll help assemble, all right? We should heat up the sour kraut separately.

(They get busy. **ARTHUR** *goes to* **SYLVIA.***)*

Sylvia?

SYLVIA. Good for you, Arthur.

ARTHUR. What?

SYLVIA. You think I don't see it?

ARTHUR. What, honey?

SYLVIA. That superior smirk.

ARTHUR. I didn't…

SYLVIA. Well, just wait. See how superior you are when we're gone. When you're left here alone.

ARTHUR. I don't want to be left alone, Sylvia. I want to be with you.

SYLVIA. It's fine to do that in front of me. Make fun of it. But don't ruin it for Rachel.

ARTHUR. Honey. It was an electrical storm. I'm sorry, I'm sorry I didn't…But I knew. That it was a storm. That it would pass over.

SYLVIA. You'll see.

ARTHUR. I love you, Sylvia. Can I ask for *your* forgiveness? Can I repent for *you*?

SYLVIA. *(brokenhearted)* It won't get you saved.

ARTHUR. I feel like I am saved.

SYLVIA. You're not.

ARTHUR. I feel like I'm waking up. All these years. I know I kind of checked out. You needed me and…I wasn't there. For a long time. I know. It's crazy, but I forgot why I was here. Even before the attacks, even before that. I'd forgotten. What I really cared about. But I remember now.

*(***RACHEL** *and* **NELSON** *have stopped their Reuben preparations to listen.* **ARTHUR** *searches for the right words.)*

I don't have faith like you have, Sylvia. I'm concrete.

You know that. I like proof. I like facts. Even when I used to go to temple, it was never about faith or God. It was about my father, my grandfather. There was only one time in my life I had real faith. It was when I fell in love with you. When we got married – we didn't even know each other that well – but I knew. I knew that whatever happened I could take it. We could take it. If we were together. That I wanted to face whatever happened with you.

I know I let you down, Sylvia. Please forgive me. Please take me back.

SYLVIA. I'm going to lose you again.

ARTHUR. But could we be together now? Whatever time I have left with you? Even if it's only a few more hours. Could we just give up on me for eternity – I'm a lost cause for eternity. But could I be with you now?

(*She looks at him. A rush of memories comes back. She goes to him. He wraps his arms around her.*)

ARTHUR. Thank you. This could last me. I love you, Honey.

(*Pause.* **ARTHUR** *looks up and sees* **RACHEL** *and* **NELSON** *waiting, quietly.*)

ARTHUR. Should we get moving on those Reubens?

SYLVIA. (*gives him a kiss*) I want mine first so I can have my brownie.

NELSON. Yes!

(*Light shift.* **RACHEL**, **NELSON**, **ARTHUR** *and* **SYLVIA** *are all playing Hearts.* **NELSON** *throws a card.*)

SYLVIA. Okay. Now see why that wasn't a good choice, Nelson? If you're going to keep the queen, you should have kept the other high spades. You see? So that if someone throws low spades, you won't get stuck with the queen.

RACHEL. Unless you're planning on taking them all.

NELSON. I love this game.

RACHEL. You've lost every time! You're terrible.

SYLVIA. He's learning. Do you want to take that card back?

RACHEL. No! We already know what he has then. No take backsies.

SYLVIA. Oh my gosh. I remember that. No take backsies.

ARTHUR. They're ferocious chess players, Nelson. You don't want to step in the chess ring with them.

RACHEL. *(to NELSON)* Do you play?

NELSON. I never tried.

RACHEL. I'll teach you. Where's the board, Mom?

SYLVIA. We probably never unpacked it. All the boxes are in the cellar.

RACHEL. Let's unpack!

SYLVIA. Well…there's really no sense to it. I mean…we're not going to be here much longer.

RACHEL. I want to unpack.

SYLVIA. I have no idea where you'd find it. There are a lot of boxes.

(putting down her last card)

Tada!

RACHEL. Oh my God, Mom.

NELSON. You're an awesome, unstoppable, winning machine, Mrs. S. It's like you *are* the cards.

RACHEL. Deal again! I'm going to destroy you this time.

NELSON. I wish I were good at games. The only thing I know how to play is the guitar.

ARTHUR. I wish I could play guitar.

NELSON. I'll teach you if you guys teach me chess.

SYLVIA. Well. Chess takes years to learn. And we don't have…

Let's find the chess set.

RACHEL. Excellent! This is so excellent.

(She runs out to go to the cellar.)

NELSON. You want me to show you a few chords, Mr. S.? While we're waiting?

ARTHUR. Why don't you do your Torah portion for Sylvia.

NELSON. Nah.

ARTHUR. Come on. Just do that part we worked on. Show off a little.

SYLVIA. If he doesn't want to…

NELSON. Well, I do want to. I mean, if you want to hear.

ARTHUR. Good. Do it.

> (**NELSON** *does the piece he was working on. It's now perfected and very beautiful.*)

NELSON. Vayomer Elohim le-Noach ket kol-basar
ba lefanay ki-male'al ha'arets chamas
mipeneyhem vehineni mashchitam et-ha'arets.

> (**RACHEL** *comes up during this with an enormous box, still sealed with packing tape. The words "GAMES AND TOYS" is written across it.*)

> (**NELSON** *finishes. They all stand silent for a moment.*)

RACHEL. That was incredible.

ARTHUR. He's good, right?

NELSON. That's the only part I do well. Your Dad helped a ton. The rest of it kind of stinks.

RACHEL. You worked on that with him?

ARTHUR. Nah. I did nothing. We really have to get moving, Bub. You've only got another month.

NELSON. Yeah.

> (*remembering, to* **SYLVIA**)

I mean, not that we're going to be here. But if we were…

ARTHUR. I can't tell you, Nelson. I'm looking forward to your Bar Mitzvah like I haven't looked forward…in years. I have to find my good suit. It's going to swim on me. I'll have to have it taken in.

RACHEL. Doesn't he have a great voice? Mom?

SYLVIA. He does. That was beautiful.

NELSON. You're invited too, of course. Mrs. S. I mean, if we're still here.

SYLVIA. (*pause*) I would like that. I would be proud to come.

RACHEL. *(the box)* Let's rip this open. It's a miracle I found it. I mean, did we unpack anything when we moved? I'm surprised we're not all naked and shoeless.

SYLVIA. It was all pretty fast. I guess we never really got to everything.

RACHEL. *(opening the box)* Hello time capsule from our murky past.

(She begins taking out board games and some dolls and a princess dress.)

NELSON. You played with dolls, Rachel? I can't picture it.

RACHEL. Twister!

NELSON. *(a princess dress)* You wore this?

SYLVIA. You were so sweet in that.

RACHEL. Cinderella was my Elvis.

NELSON. I would love to see you in this dress.

RACHEL. Yeah, I bet you would.

(taking things out)

God. Who were these people?

ARTHUR. I don't know.

RACHEL. Chess! Yay!

(She pulls it out.)

Come on Mom. I'll take you first. Here. Sit with me Nelson. I'll show you how the master plays.

(They move around the table.)

ARTHUR. I'm going to get some snacks together.

RACHEL. *(noticing the time)* Wow. School was over hours ago. We missed our social studies quiz.

(pause)

Oh well. This is really fun. I'm glad we're doing this.

(She gives her mom a hug. SYLVIA is stunned.)

Come on. Don't be chicken, Mom. I'll make it short and painless.

(They sit down to chess.)

(Light shift. Night. **RACHEL** *and* **SYLVIA** *are back at the chessboard.* **ARTHUR** *sits reading The Times.)*

SYLVIA. You've got to look ahead.

RACHEL. I did look ahead.

SYLVIA. You have to look further ahead.

RACHEL. I looked further ahead.

SYLVIA. Checkmate!

RACHEL. Nooo! That's it! My head hurts from losing. Your turn, Dad.

ARTHUR. You know I'll lose. I always lose.

RACHEL. Good. I'll play you after. Hey where's Nelson?

SYLVIA. He was just here.

ARTHUR. Must be in the loo.

*(***ARTHUR** *goes to the table with* **SYLVIA** *and they begin setting up for another game.)*

Go easy on me, Hon.

*(***RACHEL** *flops down on the sofa.* **STEPHEN HAWKING** *rolls in beside her.)*

RACHEL. Jesus Christ! You scared the hell out of me!

STEPHEN. Your house is not very wheelchair accessible.

RACHEL. What are you doing here? I'm not smoking any more.

STEPHEN. Maybe I'm a flashback.

RACHEL. It's very freaky having you here in my living room.

STEPHEN. Imagine what it's like for me.

RACHEL. Yeah.

(pause)

Listen. Stephen. We need to talk.

STEPHEN. Uh oh.

RACHEL. I've learned so much from you, you know? I think you're just great and brilliant and inspiring and your book has basically changed my life.

STEPHEN. Are you dumping me?

RACHEL. No, no. But Nelson's helping me learn about the universe now, and I have a lot of reading to do – I mean, I should see some other astrophysicists' and cosmologists' work.

STEPHEN. You're seeing other astrophysicists?

RACHEL. Just to get a broad scope, you know? And really, you must have better things to do than hang out in the suburbs with a sixteen-year-old girl.

STEPHEN. Here it is – the bum's rush.

RACHEL. No. You saved me. You really did.

STEPHEN. But don't let the door hit you on the way out.

RACHEL. I feel like I know what I want now. What I want to do. I think if I work like crazy on the math, really keep at it for the next twenty years or so, I'll probably never come up with the ground-breaking, wild ideas, but I might at least be able to understand them. That's worth living for, right?

STEPHEN. No. I think you should come up with the ground-breaking, wild ideas.

RACHEL. Yeah?

STEPHEN. And then prove it with the math.

RACHEL. Okay.

STEPHEN. *(He begins wheeling out.)* And work on the chess. Your endgame stinks. You're embarrassing yourself.

RACHEL. Okay. Thanks.

(He's gone.)

Nelson!!!

ARTHUR. Your mother is killing me, Rachel. Brings back old times.

RACHEL. Where is he?

(calling out)

Yo! Steinberg! Hurry it up. I need to play someone I can beat.

SYLVIA. Take that move back. I'm three moves from mate.

ARTHUR. Ohhh.

RACHEL. He was just here playing guitar. Wasn't he?

(She goes offstage. We hear her calling to him in different areas of the house. She reenters.)

He's not here.

SYLVIA. What?

ARTHUR. You checked both bathrooms?

RACHEL. I looked all over.

SYLVIA. *(calling)* Nelson?

ARTHUR. That's strange.

RACHEL. His guitar is still here, so he can't be far.

ARTHUR. Maybe he ran home for something.

RACHEL. *(looking out the window)* The lights are off across the street.

ARTHUR. Maybe you should call.

RACHEL. It's late Dad.

SYLVIA. Oh no. What time is it?

RACHEL. It's almost twelve.

SYLVIA. Oh my God. The day's almost over. How did I lose track? We should have been praying – preparing.

RACHEL. *(calling outside)* Nelson!
Where could he be? I've never seen him go anywhere without his guitar.

SYLVIA. It's happened. He's been taken.

ARTHUR. He'll be right back.

RACHEL. Wouldn't he say? If he were going out?

SYLVIA. *(turning on the TV to check)* Oh Lord. It's happening. Nelson's been taken.

ARTHUR. Maybe we should call him. Try information.

RACHEL. I hate to wake them up. They don't sound all that friendly.

SYLVIA. Jesus. It's time isn't it?

RACHEL. This is so weird.

(into the phone)

Steinberg.

Ummm…. Do you remember his stepdad's name?

ARTHUR. It started with a B. Bob?

RACHEL. *(back to the phone)* I don't know. But they're on Travis Street. Number 81.

SYLVIA. I love you, Jesus. But please take us all. Don't leave Rachel and Arthur.

RACHEL. Mom, it's not the Rapture.

(the TV)

Look, the news is all about the war. Nothing about people disappearing.

(into the phone)

That would be great, thanks.

SYLVIA. Or was Nelson the only one of us good enough to be taken?

RACHEL. *(the phone)* There's no answer. It's the machine.

SYLVIA. *(falling apart)* Jesus, help me.

RACHEL. His stepfather is Ben. Ben and Crystal Steinberg.

SYLVIA. Without you here, I don't know. I don't understand.

RACHEL. They don't even mention Nelson on the machine.

(She hangs up. **SYLVIA** *grabs the phone.)*

SYLVIA. I'll call Justine Knox. She was there at the start of Blessed Name. If anything happened…It's the machine. She's been taken. She and Michael.

ARTHUR. It's very late. Maybe they're asleep.

*(**SYLVIA** is madly dialing again.)*

SYLVIA. They were all taken. We weren't chosen.

RACHEL. Mom, nothing has happened. We haven't heard anything.

ARTHUR. No trumpets, Honey. The stars are still in the sky.

SYLVIA. Reverend Peter isn't answering. He's gone. They're all gone.

*(**SYLVIA** sits distraught. **RACHEL** goes to her. Puts her arms around her.)*

RACHEL. It's all right, Mom. It's going to be all right.

SYLVIA. I couldn't save any of us. I couldn't do it. I'm not strong enough.

ARTHUR. Sylvia. You are strong. You're a good person. You do good in the world.

SYLVIA. I do?

ARTHUR. And I'll help you. From now on I will. You kept asking me, and I wouldn't come. But I will. I'll come to the shelter with you, and I'll do all the good…works with you. The soup kitchen. Whatever you do. I'll help.

SYLVIA. It's almost midnight. Two minutes.

RACHEL. It's going to be okay, Mom. I'm sorry – I'm really sorry I was such a shit to you. And I'll stop saying shit. I'll stop saying all the terrible things I say. It's going to be okay now. It is.

(They all three hold onto each other. The church bell begins chiming twelve times.)

(There is a loud crash outside.)

RACHEL. Holy…. What was that?

SYLVIA. Jesus? Are you coming for us?

(Pause. They all listen for a response.)

Jesus. I'm sorry. But I'm not sorry. I can't go unless you take us all. I need to be here with my family. I need to stay here – even if it's hell on Earth.

ARTHUR. I love you so much. Both of you.

(NELSON bursts in.)

NELSON. I got the water chestnuts!

(They all stare at him dumbfounded.)

The Shoprite was open. I thought I'd surprise you. It really is better with the water chestnuts.

It was kind of amazing going out without my outfit. Nobody verbally or physically abused me. In fact, one woman complimented me on my handsome belt.

Is everything okay?

RACHEL. DON'T YOU EVER DO THAT AGAIN!

NELSON. What?

RACHEL. Don't you ever go anywhere without telling me again. You hear me? You scared the life out of all of us. Don't you ever do that again.

NELSON. Okay.

(She goes to him and throws her arms around him. He hugs her tight. Then he takes her face in his hands and kisses her.)

ARTHUR. Huh. I was almost convinced. I couldn't imagine never seeing him again.

SYLVIA. Wednesday is over.

He didn't come.

NELSON. Maybe it wasn't supposed to be this Wednesday.

RACHEL. Don't, Nelson.

SYLVIA. I'm going to miss him. So much.

NELSON. Maybe we should wait next Wednesday, just in case.

ARTHUR. I would do that.

SYLVIA. How could I have been wrong? Was I crazy?

NELSON. I don't think you were crazy, Mrs. S.

RACHEL. Mom. Is this so bad? If this is all there is? Even if there is no eternity. No one in charge. If all we have is this. Us. And one short lifetime. It's not so bad.

SYLVIA. I don't know how to do this any more. I've been preparing for the end…I don't know…

RACHEL. We'll have to figure it out.

NELSON. Maybe he'll still come. I think we should keep waiting. Every Wednesday. Maybe he'll still come.

(They sit together, contemplating this, as lights slowly fade.)

(Lights down.)

End of Play

From the Reviews of
END DAYS...

"Perhaps only Deborah Zoe Laufer would think to combine a Goth girl, her born-again mom, her post-9/11 depressed dad, an Elvis-loving neighbor, Jesus, and Stephen Hawking in the same play – and make the combination hilarious...a rapturously funny play about a family trying to survive in a world hurtling toward Armageddon, *[End Days]* proves that the right playwright can inspire healing laughter in even the most sobering subjects."
– *The Miami Herald*

"A satirical dark comedy with a moral edge. The universality of the denouement brings this comedy full circle, leaving us to admire the relevancy of Laufer's humor and wisdom of her message."
– *Variety*

"...Both poignantly redemptive and often hilariously funny. I hope others will have the opportunity to see this special play. It begs the question of what we would hold most sacred if we knew the end was near. And it brings to life our broad range of choices, including laughter, and the treasured traveling companions who are there even when we face our own personal Armageddon."
– *Huffington Post*

"*End Days* may be about a weirdly dysfunctional family that finds its soul by waiting for the Apocalypse together, but this play has heart: It's engaging, funny as hell and even touching....An exceptional show"
– *NUVO (Indianapolis)*

"A manic whirlwind of a family drama as weird and illuminating and truthful as anything likely to be discovered at CERN. *End Days* is funnier than a great many plays designed solely to induce laughter, and more touching than most plays designed solely to touch...so redolent of the ordinary wishes of real, lonely human beings that, despite the play's atmosphere of general absurdity, it communicates a heartbreaking truthfulness."
– *Broward-Palm Beach New Times*

"...thought-provoking, not a little disquieting and seriously, encouragingly funny. Laufer's originality in expressing her ideas is impressive. Highly recommended."
– *CityBeat Arts and Entertainment*

"The smartest, most hysterical, laugh-out-loud show you'll see in the theater - ever! ...a witty, funny AND relevant play."
– *Martha's Vineyard Plum*

"*End Days* directly pits science, religion and suburbia, but it's not an attack on any of them. There's not a trace of mockery in these extraordinary performances, each tinged with compassion, humor and heartbreak. Laufer is clearly a major new voice"
– *Denver Post*

Also by
Deborah Zoe Laufer...

The Last Schwartz

Out of Sterno

Please visit our website **samuelfrench.com** for complete
descriptions and licensing information

CPSIA information can be obtained
at www.ICGtesting.com
Printed in the USA
BVHW01s1937271117
501338BV00007B/135/P